ELIZABETH NYE

TITANIC SURVIVOR

Elizabeth Nye

TITANIC
SURVIVOR

A Biography by Dave Bryceson

Streets
Publishers

Foreword by General John Gowans (R)

Published by
Streets Publishers,
'Richmond', Poplar Drive, Stotfold, Hitchin, Herts SG5 4AF
England

Copyright © 2009 Streets Publishers and Dave Bryceson

ISBN: 978-0-9561054-0-0

Designed and Printed in England by
Streets Printers Ltd
Royston Road, Baldock, Herts SG7 6NW
Cover: Chris Brown Design

*Elizabeth, centre back row, taking part in
a children's tableau presentation.*

CONTENTS

DEDICATION

This book is dedicated to the memory of Elizabeth, a fellow Folkestonian. During her upbringing in Folkestone as Lizzie Ramell, and during her first marriage and emigration to the New World as Elizabeth Nye, fate threw in her path every conceivable cruel obstacle it could muster. Throughout, with her faith in God, her love of caring for others and her sense of humour, she rose above it all and, in New York City and Belmar, New Jersey, as Mrs Bess Darby, an Officer of The Salvation Army, she devoted the remainder of her life to God and to the service of others. She was truly an example to us all. My research into Elizabeth's life has led me to develop great admiration and respect for her and the organisation for which she worked. One of the contributors I contacted during my enquiries ended her reply, 'Thank you for making our lives more interesting'.

It wasn't me, it was Elizabeth. Her legacy lives on.

* **The sum of £1.00, or local equivalent, from the sale of each copy of this book will be donated to support the work of the Salvation Army.**

Also by Dave Bryceson

THE TITANIC DISASTER

As Reported in the British National Press April-July 1912

UK Edition:	Patrick Stephens Ltd., Sparkford, Somerset, BA22 7JJ *ISBN 1 85260 579 0*
US Edition:	W. W. Norton & Company Inc., 500 Fifth Avenue, New York, NY 10110 Library of Congress Ref G530.T6B79 1997 *ISBN 0 393 04108 5*

FOREWORD

BY GENERAL JOHN GOWANS

INTERNATIONAL LEADER OF THE SALVATION ARMY
(July 1999 - November 2002)

The Folkestone Corps will live on in Salvationist folk memory around the world for as long as there is a Salvation Army. The early days of the Army in that seaside resort town seemed to encapsulate all that was best about the Movement: the courage of the pioneers, their single-mindedness, their goodness and love, and the simplicity of their faith. High amongst those heroes stood Bandmaster Tom Ramell.

I am delighted to be able to recommend this book, which recounts the life-story of Elizabeth Ramell, the worthy daughter of Bandmaster Tom. Elizabeth Ramell, nurtured and trained by the all-too-human saints of the Folkestone Corps, went on to serve God as a Salvation Army soldier and officer in three countries, was bereaved of a loving husband and daughter, and, the event that dominated her early womanhood, was a survivor of the sinking of the Titanic. Her qualities of faith, caring concern and perseverance, along with a good sense of humour and a strong dash of common sense, ensure that the story of her life is not that of some pathetic victim of fate, but is uplifting and positive to a marked degree.

I am sure that the readers will enjoy this book, and find something in the story of Elizabeth Ramell, latterly Mrs Colonel George Darby, to encourage them in their own daily journey through the changing landscapes of their lives.

We are most grateful to Dave Bryceson, a good friend of the Army, for his labour of love in bringing this story to light and making it available for our pleasure and benefit. I wish especially to thank him for his generosity in donating to Army funds, £1 from the sale of each book.

John Gowans
General (R)

'THE PAPERS NEVER TELL THE RIGHT NEWS'

Some years ago when my interest in the story of the *Titanic* disaster of 1912 was first awakened by repeated viewings of the movies, '*A Night to Remember*' and '*S.O.S. Titanic*', I received some advice from a fellow enthusiast. He told me that the most detailed personal accounts of the disaster were to be found in local newspaper reports rather than the national press of the time. It was superb advice that I had no way of knowing then was to set me off on a nineteen-year quest on both sides of the Atlantic.

Asked to name *Titanic* survivors from memory, I suspect that many of we enthusiasts would be able to list perhaps the twenty or so most high-profile passengers who later wrote books or who were often mentioned or quoted in newspaper articles. There would remain of course 685 survivors who, for whatever their reasons, rarely, if ever, spoke out publicly about their experiences.

One such survivor was second-class passenger Elizabeth Nye. I first became aware of her story whilst searching through the 1912 archive editions of the *Folkestone Express, Sandgate, Shorncliffe and Hythe Advertiser*, stored on microfiche at the Folkestone Library. I had been primarily looking for advertisements for a bioscope show that had been touring the United Kingdom about the tragedy when I chanced across this article in the 20th April edition:

LOST TITANIC

FOLKSTONIAN AMONG THE SAVED

There will probably arrive to-day some reliable news as to the terrible catastrophe which during the week has so largely occupied the thoughts of everybody in this country. The loss of life through the sinking of the monster ship was reported yesterday to be even larger than was at first thought, the liner Carpathia having less than eight hundred of the saved on board.

One of the second-class passengers, whose name appears in the list of saved, is Mrs Elizabeth Nye, who is a widow, and the daughter of Mr Ramell, coach-builder of Dover Road. Mrs Nye had originally intended to sail in another ship, which, owing to the coal strike, did not leave dock, and she was transferred to the Titanic. She was an officer of the Salvation Army and has gone to New York to take up duty there. Her husband, who died about a year ago, was also an officer of the Salvation Army. Mr Ramell was in great fear when the news of the Titanic arrived that his daughter was among the drowned, but to his great relief he found her name among the rescued.

A brother of Mr Wood, postmaster, of Hythe, is reported to be among the lost. He was one of the stewards.

The 1st May 1912 edition contained this article about the bioscope show:

'FOLKESTONE ELECTRIC THEATRE RENDEZVOUS STREET - TITANIC DISASTER. A series of pictures of Extraordinary Interest is expected to arrive in England from New York in the course of a day or two, and will be shown immediately on arrival.'

Once the slides were here, the wording in subsequent advertisements was changed to, 'Including the following scenes:- Captain Smith on the Bridge. The Graveyard of the Sea. Icebergs and Iceflows in the neighbourhood of the Disaster. The Carpathia nearing New York with Survivors. Some Survivors of the Titanic's Crew. Their Last Resting Place.'

When the same show moved to the cinema on the Pier their curiously worded advertisement read, 'SUNDAY PICTURES AT THE PIER PAVILION - The programme arranged for to-morrow at 3 and 8 will be of a very attractive nature, including 18 scenes dealing with the *Titanic* Disaster.' 'Attractive' - Hardly an adjective that the 705 *Titanic* survivors would have used to describe their traumatic experience. However, when I scrolled down below that entry to the Saturday, 4th May edition, I was delighted to find this follow-up article relating to Elizabeth Nye:

THE TITANIC DISASTER

FOLKESTONE SURVIVOR'S STORY
MRS NYE'S CLEAR NARRATIVE

As was reported a fortnight ago; there was one Folkestone passenger on the Titanic at the time that vessel collided with the iceberg, and fortunately she was saved. Mrs Elizabeth Nye, daughter of Mr and Mrs Ramell of 64, Dover Road, was on her way back to America, where she was going to take up an appointment under the Salvation Army. Mrs Nye is a widow, her husband, a Folkestone man, having died in America. She came home last year again, but decided to return to the States, and it was really owing to the coal strike that she was on board the ill-fated vessel, for she should have sailed a week previously. She was a second class passenger on the Titanic, and news of her rescue was the greatest relief and gratification to her parents and relatives, and her many friends in the town. Mr and Mrs Ramell have been inundated with congratulations at their daughter's safety, and they have been deeply touched by the many kind messages received by them.

Mrs Elizabeth Nye.

They were not aware they had so many friends, and the letters and telegrams received included some from friends in Paris, London, Tunbridge Wells and many other towns. They desire to express their thanks to the hundreds of friends who were so solicitous in the trying time they have recently undergone.

The news of Mrs Nye's rescue was received on the Tuesday after the collision, and last week end her mother and father received a letter from her giving a description of her experiences of the night of horror, when the giant liner went down with so many hundreds of passengers and crew. Her letter, which is set out below, was written on the Carpathia on the Tuesday following the wreck, is in bold and distinct handwriting, and it is a clear narrative of what occurred. There is nothing hysterical about it; it is, in fact, a well thought out letter, written by a woman who must have been strong both in nerves and physique, and gives one of the simplest and best accounts that has appeared in the public Press.

Mrs Nye enclosed in her letter a picture postcard of the Carpathia leaving Messina, and at the back of it she wrote the words "The ship that saved my life". The letter, which will be read with great interest by her numerous friends, was as follows:-

"My dear mother and dad, I expect you have been wondering whether you would ever hear from me again. You have seen by the papers the wreck of the Titanic, but after the most terrible time of my life I am safe. My nerves are very shattered, I look and feel about ten years older, but I will get over it after a time.

You will like to hear the truth of the wreck from me, for the papers never tell the right news. We were all in bed on Sunday night at about 11.30, when we felt an awful jerk, and the boat grazed something along its side, and the sea seemed to splash right over the deck. The men in the next cabin slipped on their coats and ran up to see what it was, and came and told us the ship had run into an iceberg nearly as large as herself.

Most of the people went back to bed again, but then came an order 'get up and put something warm on, put on a lifebelt, and come on deck.' So I got one underskirt on, and a skirt, and stockings, and shoes and coat, and ran up to find a lifebelt, because there were only three in our berth for four of us. A boy from the next room stole one from ours, but he went down with it, poor boy. We did not have time to go back to our cabins again to get anything, and we did not dream it was serious. I thought I should get back to get more clothes on and get a few other things, but we were put into the lifeboats, and pushed off at once.

They put all the ladies and children in first. I guess there were 30 or 40 in our boat. It seemed to be the last one lowered with women in it.

When we got away from the ship we could understand the hurry and the order to get half a mile away as soon as possible. For the Titanic was half in the water. We watched the port-holes go under until half the ship only, the back half, stuck up. Then the lights went out, and the boilers burst and blew up. There was a sickening roar like hundreds of lions, and we heard no more but the moaning and shouting for help from the hundreds of men and a few women who went down with her.

There were not enough boats for so many people. Twenty boats were lowered, and only fourteen boats were picked up. Several men were on a raft that was thrown out, and their cries for help were so pitiful for so long. Only one fellow, about 21 years old, is alive from the raft. He says the men were pushed off to make it lighter. This man was on it six hours, and then saved.

Just before the ship went down, the Captain, the same Captain Smith of the twin ship Olympic, jumped into the sea and picked up a little girl who was hanging to the ship, and put her on the raft. They pulled him on, too, but he would not stay. He said 'Good-bye, boys, I must go with the ship.' He swam back through the icy waters, and died at his post. The little girl died too.

How the few men worked on our little boat, and how they kept up, I don't know. We were drifting among the icebergs for hours, and, oh, it was so cold. We had not enough clothes on. I had no blouse, and others had no stockings or underclothes. The boat rocked so, and made me seasick. There were three or four young babies there without their mothers. How they screamed!

We were all perished with cold, drifting along, looking for

a vessel of some kind and waiting for the dawn. We sighted a bright light soon, and we all watched it so anxiously. It came along closer and closer, til we saw more lights on her and knew that help was at hand. The suspense was terrible. We were afraid they did not know of the wreck, or that they would not see our lights, for most of the boats had no light, only a lighted rope end. We had no drink or provision. The only thing in our favour was the clear starlight night and fairly smooth sea.

This boat, the Carpathia, of the Cunard line, was going from Halifax to Berlin. She was the only ship near enough to catch the wireless message for help from the Titanic, and then the operator says he was just leaving and closing the door, when he heard the clicking of the wireless. So it was taken just in time, for they never sent another message, and it was an hour and a quarter after that before the first lifeboat got to the ship. Of course, she stood still, and waited for us all to come up. They were all in but two when we got in.

We were in the little boat for just five hours and a half before being rescued.

They lowered bags for the babies to pull them up, and we sat on a kind of swing and were drawn up by rope to safety. They have been most kind to us. Led us one by one to the dining room, and gave us brandy. I drank half a glass of brandy down without water. We were all perished, and it put life into us. The ship is, of course, filled with its own passengers. But they found places for us all to sleep, but none of us slept well after going through such a horrible nightmare.

This ship stood right over the place where the Titanic went down, and picked us up. Two small boats were picked up later. They were floating. One had seven dead bodies in it, and the other just a dead boatman. They sewed them up in canvas here, weighted them, and gave them a Christian burial at sea. Two small boats filled with passengers capsized. They all went down but two or three, who clung to the up-turned boat, and were saved.

We are told that the SS Baltic picked up about fifty men, and the poor women here are hoping their husbands are among the fifty. It is supposed there are 160 more widows through this wreck, and most of them have children. It was so heart-breaking to see and hear them crying for their husbands.

We were all gathered together, and our names taken for the newspapers. Of course, they cannot tell how many are dead, but we have on this ship only two hundred crew out of 910, and 500 passengers out of 2,000. I am amongst the fortunate, for God has spared my life when I was so near to death again. I have lost everything I had on board. The only thing that I saved was my watch Dad gave me eleven years ago.

But all my treasures and clothes, and even some money have gone down. I only have the scanty clothes I stand up in, including my big coat, which has been such a blessing.

We expect to land on Wednesday night, or next morning. I shall be so thankful, for I feel so ill on this boat. The boat is not so nice and we have to sleep in the bottom of the boat. But still, I thank God I am alive.

I could tell you much more of the horrors of Sunday night, but will write again later on land. I can't bear to think of it all now. Will you let Auntie and Edie see this and tell all my friends I am safe. You must have all been anxious.

With fondest love to all, from

"Lizzie"

A similar report together with the letter and photograph appeared in the *Folkestone, Hythe, Sandgate and Cheriton Herald,* and a third local paper, the *Folkestone Daily News*, a broadsheet, also published a short report.

Cunarder Carpathia *leaving Messina - an identical postcard to that sent by Elizabeth to her parents.*
(Geoff Robinson Collection)

After learning that there had been a survivor from the *Titanic* from my own hometown I determined to find out as much as I could about Elizabeth Nye and her family. The quest had begun . . .

'KEEP THE BAND INDOORS UNTIL THEY CAN PLAY!'

The Folkestone Library Heritage Centre was able to assist with a number of my enquiries, and further help was to come from an unexpected source when, after adding a photograph of Elizabeth to my annual *Titanic* window display, one of my regular customers announced that he was Elizabeth's great nephew. I am indebted to John Dalton and his father Jack, for their permission to use a number of photographs from their family albums throughout this book.

Elizabeth's father, Thomas Ingram Ramell, was born in Lambeth, South London in 1855. His childhood had not been a happy one as his father, Barnard Ramell a plasterer, was often away from home and Thomas had to remain in the house with his mother who was an alcoholic.

When Thomas was eleven he was no doubt delighted when his parents accepted an offer for him to go and live with his uncle, Frederick Ingram Ramell, in the seaside town of Folkestone, Kent in the south east of England. Frederick was a master carriage manufacturer and apprenticed Thomas into the firm, initially teaching him the skill of a carriage painter.

An 1884 receipt from Ramell & Son, Carriage Builders.

Carriage built by Messrs Ramell, of Dover Road, for Sir Israel Hart, Liberal candidate for the Borough in 1900. The carriage was painted in Liberal Blue.

(Folkestone Library Heritage Centre Collection.)

So prestigious were the carriages that the Ramells made, that the firm was awarded the honour of repairing and painting the carriages of the

Prince of Wales. The Carriage Works, at 15-21 Dover Road, were duly decorated with the Royal Coat of Arms marking the Royal Appointment. Beneath this appeared the inscription, 'Universal Providers of Every Description of High Class Carriages'. The buildings which housed the works remained in existence until 1995 when they were demolished to make way for a new medical centre. Right up to the time of demolition the main building could still be identified by the 'Bulls Eyes' window glass which had survived all those years.

The Ramell Carriage Factory, circa 1910.
(Folkestone Library Heritage Centre Collection.)

The same building just prior to its demolition in 1995.
(Author's Collection.)

On 26th August 1877, at the age of 23, Thomas married a local girl, Elizabeth Ann Griffiths, also 23 and the daughter of John Griffiths, a professional fossil collector. The couple took lodgings at 4 Foord Road, just a short walk from the Carriage Works. On 27th May 1882, the same year in which the Salvation Army began its presence in the town, Elizabeth was

Elizabeth Ramell, one year old, 1883.
(Jerilyn Sunlin Collection.)

born at home. A birth notice appeared in the 3rd June edition of the Kentish Express and Ashford News, which read:

'May 27, at 4 Foord-road, Folkestone, the wife of Thomas Ramell, of a daughter.'

The Ramells had lost two children born prior to Elizabeth and when she in turn, as a youngster, came close to death with appendicitis the couple became desperate. They were visited by a Salvation Army Captain who, on hearing of Elizabeth's condition, asked if she might be left alone with the child in order to pray. As she was later departing Thomas pronounced that if Elizabeth lived he would leave the Military Volunteer Movement with whom he was a cornet player in the Band, and join the Salvation Army. Elizabeth made a complete recovery and in time became the eldest of five daughters of the family.

With Elizabeth's recovery assured Thomas remained true to his word and became one of the early converts to the Salvation Army in Folkestone. It was at his instigation that the local Commander responded to an advertisement in 'The War Cry' reading 'Nine brass instruments £18, including a drum'.

After some hard work the money was raised and the instruments were purchased. Thomas was the only one with any knowledge of how to play them and was therefore appointed Bandmaster. The instruments were handed out according to age and size and practice began.

The Band's first appearance on the streets of Folkestone was met the following day with a message from the Town Mayor. He wrote that he was full of sympathy with the intentions of the Army but, 'would they please keep the Band indoors until they had learned to play!' There followed a further fortnight of intense practise before they felt confident enough to sally forth once more.

During the Army's first few years in Folkestone their good intentions towards the town's down-and-outs were treated with suspicion by many people. A group of local fishermen calling themselves, like similar groups around the country who were intent on destroying the Salvation Army, 'The Skeleton Army', saw fit to taunt and even assault Army members whenever they saw them. Local grocers and fishmongers would give away their rotting produce for use as missiles. At one stage the windows of the Bradstone Road Barracks had to remain boarded up for eighteen months as a precaution against attacks from the thugs.

A local clergyman offered a cash prize for the first rough to capture the army standard, 'a bastard flag that represents nothing and nobody'. Even the local press failed to understand the motives of the Salvationists as can be gleaned from the following extracts from an article that appeared in *The Folkestone Express* on 27th January 1883:

THE RIVAL ARMY NUISANCE

There seems to be no sign of an abatement of the annoyance to which the inhabitants have been subject since the "Salvation Army" obtained quarters here. Last Sunday the lower or eastern end of the town was in a state of commotion all day, in consequence of an anticipated collision between the roughs who compose the two armies - the "Skeletons" and the "Salvationists." It appears that on the preceding Sunday the "Salvationists" took possession of an open space at the extreme end of the Stade, known as "Frog Hole", which the "Skeletons" since their organisation, have appropriated to themselves as a place of rendezvous.

The intruders were quickly ousted, but it was reported that they intended to take possession on the following Sunday, and hold an open air service.

Whether there was any foundation for this rumour we are unable to say, but at all events, the "Skeletons" determined, if their rivals did put in an appearance, to give them a warm reception. To this end they procured an old gun which they loaded to the muzzle with flour and soot, putting a sufficient quantity of gunpowder in the breech to cause the flour and soot to be belched forth over any advancing foe. Further, a huge tub containing the heads of dog-fish, and other offal, which no doubt would have been freely used had opportunity offered, was provided, and the Union Jack from a pole planted close by the gun. If the "Salvationists" had ever entertained any intention of attacking the "Skeletons" stronghold, they wisely abandoned it, but nevertheless crowds of people hung about in anticipation of a skirmish.

The "Salvation" Army, however, left the Bradstone Hall soon after ten o'clock, with the intention of parading the streets in the neighbourhood of their headquarters. At the end of Queen Street they halted, and commenced a sort of service. The residents objected to their presence, and a detachment of the "Skeletons" coming up at the moment, a most disgraceful scene ensued, bags of soot and flour and other more objectionable articles being used to cause the "Salvationists" to disperse, which they did, and as soon as they could extricate themselves from the crowd, returned to Barracks, from which they ventured out no more that day in a body.

Meanwhile the main body of the "Skeletons" remained near the Harbour anxiously expecting the arrival of the other army. Shortly before eleven the eager listeners heard a body approaching shouting "We'll roll the old chariot along," and shouts of "They're coming", were heard in all directions. Suddenly, from all the many avenues which lead into the lower end of Tontine Street, men and boys were hurrying by hundreds, and in a very few minutes a dense mass consisting principally of the fishing class of the community, and labouring men, effectually barred the street. Nearer and nearer came the sound of the advancing party, and at a shout of, "fall in", the expectant "Skeletons" ranged themselves in ranks extending from one side of the road to the other. There were growls of disappointment and roars of laughter, when it was discovered that what was supposed to be the "Salvationists" was only the detachment of the "Skeletons" who were returning from their "brush" in John Street, elated with victory. On they came, shouting at the top of their voices, turning up High Street, and down the Dover Road, to the Bradstone Hall, outside which building they hooted, groaned and cheered, and then dispersed.

In the afternoon, a Mr Hall, a minister who lends his countenance and support to the "Salvation Army" was assailed in Tontine Street, and for about an hour disgraceful proceedings, almost amounting to rioting, ensued, flour and soot being freely thrown about.

On Monday evening there was another "scrimmage." The "Skeletons" mustered in force at headquarters, preparatory to making their nightly parade, clad in the most grotesque uniforms, and carrying many banners. The "protection of the law" is extended to the "Salvation Army" and in their perambulations they are preceded by a member of the borough police force. Not to be outdone in this respect, the "Skeletons" have procured an old police uniform, and in this they array one of their members, who stalks at their head. Before the order to march was given on Monday night, a scout brought intelligence that the "Salvationists" were out, and had gone in the direction of Sandgate Road. Away went the "Skeletons" helter skelter up the High Street, hoping to meet the other army near the Town Hall. But they too had scouts, who warned them of what was coming, and they at once made in hot haste to their "barracks." Down Rendezvous Street and Dover Road the "Skeletons" were close at their heels, and overtook them just as they turned into Bradstone Road. Like a flock of frightened sheep they fled on, but the Philistines, in the shape of the Skeletons, were upon them, and for a few minutes the two armies were mingled. No violence was used, but one of the officers of the "Salvationists" seized hold of the captain of the Skeletons, who, however, quickly disengaged himself and the men under his orders reformed and marched away, "Rolling the chariot along."

The foregoing is the state of things which the Salvation Army has been the means of inflicting upon Folkestone, all the appeals which have been made to them to discontinue their obnoxious processions having been treated with contempt, notwithstanding the fact that the authorities have actually gone out of their way in order that their services indoors may be uninterrupted. And yet in the face of this there are found men in a good social position, who would be foremost in arraigning the authorities, under any other circumstances, for not preserving order in the streets, who support those peacebreakers.

We are always extremely chary in any remarks we may make relating to any body of persons having the remotest claim to be a religious sect. In religious politics we advocate the fullest freedom, every man and woman being entitled to enjoy his or her own opinion, but when the members of any sect come outside their licensed premises, and by their misconduct disturb the peace of the inhabitants and destroy their comfort, then we do not hesitate to denounce their proceedings and we must look for and question their motives.

We hear of young women who have been led away by their "religious enthusiasm" as it is called, handing over their savings to furnish the apartments of the "captains," "lieutenants" and others connected with the army, who evidently appreciate the good things of this life, though they induce these poor dupes to

> sacrifice them in the hope of being repaid in another world. What will be the state of these weakminded girls, when they recover from the "paroxysms of enthusiasm" into which, as we read in an account of a "hallelujah meeting" at Salisbury, many of them work themselves? How terrible will be the reaction when, having been "drunk with the new wine and reeled about the streets in the ecstasy of their intoxication," they sit clothed in their right minds and contemplate the social ruin to which they have been reduced?
>
> The end must come; let us hope it will be before much more mischief is done.

Eventually an end to the opposition and mistrust did come but it was to take a number of years. The Ramell sisters would have witnessed many unpleasant scenes during their formative years before the Folkestone Corps was allowed to function unhindered. The good work of the Salvation Army continues in this town today.

For the band, once the instruments were mastered, it was time to turn their attention to their appearance. The problem of headgear was solved by a local clothier who sold, for one shilling each, military pith helmets that had been discarded by the troops returning from the Sudan. The Army had not finalised an official uniform by this time, so Thomas designed himself a rather splendiferous jacket. To identify himself further as the leader of the band, Thomas was the only member allowed to wear white gloves during their concerts. He was later to become revered in Salvation Army circles as, 'Bandmaster Tom'. The Army operated from the same premises in Bradstone Road until June 2002. Later that year a new, purpose-built Church and Community Centre was opened in Canterbury Road.

The 1891 UK Census lists the Ramell family as by that time living at 42 St Johns Street. Elizabeth was then eight years of age, Edith five and Beatrice two. To help with household expenses the family took in two lodgers, John Edward Smith and his son, Steven, of Peasmarsh, Sussex who were employed in Folkestone as gardeners.

With the later births of Florence and Winifred it was time to move to a larger property and in 1901 Thomas chose 64 Dover Road, a three story semi-detached house with a small enclosed and elevated rear garden. The house still stands today and is just a short walk away from my former business premises at 65 Tontine Street. I take quiet pleasure in the thought

Bandmaster Tom.
(Folkestone Library
Heritage Centre
Collection.)

The Bradstone Road Citadel.
(Author's Collection.)

that Elizabeth and her family may well have been regular visitors to the building as it was at the time the Kent and Colonial Meatstore, managed by a Mr H. Cannon, with the telephone number, Folkestone 115a!

64 Dover Road.
(Author's Collection.)

Elizabeth, like her sisters in turn after her, was schooled at Dover Road Board School where the Headmaster was a Mr E.B. Hall. Whilst the records of the sisters' individual scholastic achievements no longer exist, it is a fact that schooling for young ladies at the end of the nineteenth century centred more on domestic training such as housecraft, sewing and cookery, rather than the more academic subjects taught today. The boys and girls who attended the school were instructed in 'the three R's' - Reading, Writing and Arithmetic, and once a week an 'Object Lesson' would be taught on such diverse topics as coal, insects, an apple, travelling and bells.

I am also indebted to another descendant of the Ramell family, Clifford A. Greene L.R.A.M., A.R.C.M., son of Elizabeth's sister Florence, for much of the information about the Ramell family contained herein, including the delightful tale that as a young girl, Winifred Ramell, on her way home from school one day, decided to pay a surprise visit to her father at the Carriage Works. She crept through the workshop and suddenly burst open the door. It was she, however, who received the surprise as the only two persons present there were the bearded Prince of Wales, later to become Edward VII, earnestly engaged in conversation with a young lady!

In the late 1890s Elizabeth and Florence took part in a tableau presentation held at the Bradstone Road Citadel. Seventeen of the junior soldiers posed for this group photograph. They each wore a sailor's uniform and carried an oar and the tableau was set, prophetically for Elizabeth, in a mock-up lifeboat.

Elizabeth, centre back row. A photograph that was likely to have returned to her mind some 14 years later.
(June Fuger Collection.)

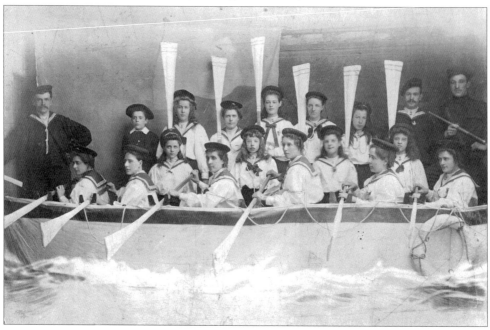

After leaving school Elizabeth gained her first employment as a dressmaker with Messrs. Musgrave and Co., Drapers and Milliners of 16-18 Sandgate Road in Folkestone. The firm specialised in 'Dresses, Costumes, Coats, Millinery, Underclothing and Corsets, Veilings, Laces, Ribbons, Silks, Trimmings etc.' An entry about Musgraves in the *Folkestone Views and Reviews* of the early 1900s reads:

'Situated in one of the leading thoroughfares of Folkestone the shop, with its double frontage, and its handsome plate glass windows, displaying to advantage a varied and artistically arranged selection of goods, bears every outward evidence of its commercial status. This is amply borne out by the interior, which is deep and lofty, admirably appointed and replete with the latest goods in each of the various departments. Amongst the more important of these may be mentioned hosiery and gloves, haberdashery, lace, furs, umbrellas, corsets, ladies underclothing, and the innumerable articles comprised under the general head of drapery. The departments devoted to millinery and to dress and mantle making call for special mention, not only from their importance as integral parts of the business, but still more for the exceptional reputation the house possesses for productions of this kind. Mr Musgrave employs a skilled and experienced staff upon the premises, and always being in the secret of the latest pronouncements of Dame Fashion, is able to provide his patrons with costumes that combine stylish and "up-to-date" design with careful and artistic workmanship'.

The dressmaking training that Elizabeth received at Musgraves was to stand her in good stead for the remainder of her life.

Musgrave Premises.
(Alan Taylor Collection.)

Press Advertisement.
(Author's Collection.)

Tragedy was to prove a constant companion to Elizabeth throughout her formative years. Her first sweetheart, Frederick John Hathill, 22 years, died on 16th December 1901, of injuries received by a fall from the

Folkestone Pier Extension Works, into the sea. The subsequent Coroners' Court was unable to find any evidence as to why the accident had occured.

There is no doubt that the Ramell household was a busy one with Tom running his business plus his commitments with the Salvation Army, activities in which his daughters were also heavily involved. One of Elizabeth's responsibilities as the eldest daughter was to run the junior Sunday School. A check of the Visitor Lists printed weekly in the local press reveals that there were often visitors staying at 64 Dover Road.

Elizabeth did however manage to find time to start 'walking out' with a local lad, Edward Ernest Nye, a non-domestic gardener who was also a member of her father's band. The couple were to fall in love. Edward, at the time, lived at 40 Canterbury Road, Folkestone and his father, William Dunster Nye, was employed as a shepherd.

One can just imagine the joy of their time spent courting whilst strolling along The Leas overlooking the English Channel where the owner, Lord Radnor, employed a uniformed private policeman, William Hudson Smith, late of the Royal Horse Guards, to keep undesirables away from The Leas as it was felt that only people of quality should be allowed to mingle there.

Postcard view of The Leas, circa 1904.
(Author's collection.)

Elizabeth's position as the daughter of a well respected manufacturer, particularly one with a Royal Appointment, would have guaranteed her the right to stroll The Leas and sit on the canopied deck-chairs to listen to the musical concerts at the Bandstand performed by 'First-class military bands, three times daily during the season.'

On more adventurous days the couple may well have visited the seafront and ridden on the Thompson's Patent Gravity Switchback wooden railway - a forerunner, and much gentler version of the rollercoasters that we know today. The Switchback is depicted on this 1912 postcard, on the reverse of which the writer, not Elizabeth but another young lady, gives a fascinating insight into the period when she wrote, "Molly and I went on this switchback the other day - it was funny. Everybody screamed but us, we remembered that we were ladies."

Postcard of the Switchback at Folkestone Seafront.
(Author's Collection.)

It is more than likely that Elizabeth and Edward experienced their first taste of Americana on Saturday, 22nd August 1903, with the exciting arrival in Folkestone of the Buffalo Bill Wild West Show.

Colonel William Cody -
Buffalo Bill.
(Author's Collection.)

Press
Advertisement.

The event, involving 800 performers and 500 horses, was staged in a 414 x 180 feet arena, surrounded by seating for 14,000 spectators. The hour and a half long show commenced with a review of the roughriders of the world led by Buffalo Bill himself - Colonel William Frederick Cody.

The remainder of the programme consisted of a portrayal of prairie life, illustrating feats of horsemanship, the use of the lasso, Indian skirmishes and tribal war dances. There were representations of the Battle of San Juan Hill, the Pony Express Mail Service and an attack on the Deadwood Stagecoach. Colonel Cody concluded the show with an impressive display of shooting from horseback. Elizabeth would have had no way of knowing at the time, of course, that within a few years she, herself would be taking part in a Salvation Army display of Americana through the streets of London.

Buffalo Bill parades in front of his cast of hundreds.
(Author's Collection.)

Back row: George Ramell, Thomas Ramell, Unknown, Edward and Elizabeth Nye, 4 x Unknown. Front row: Unknown, Elizabeth Ramell, Edith Ramell, Winifred Ramell, Unknown, Beatrice Ramell, Unknown, Florence Ramell.
(June Fuger Collection.)

On Boxing Day, 1904, at the age of 22, the brown hair and hazel-eyed Elizabeth married Edward Nye, 24, at St Michael's Church in Dover Road, Folkestone. The service was conducted by the Rev. Frederick Tapply.

The couple made their first home in rented accommodation at 15 Gladstone Road and later moved to 4 Myrtle Road, Folkestone, a small two bedroomed terrace house, just a short distance from Elizabeth's parents' home.

The Ramell Family October 1904. Edith Ramell, Mrs T. Ramell, Mr Thomas Ramell (Bandmaster Tom), Beatrice Ramell, Florence Ramell, Elizabeth Ramell, Winifred Ramell.
(Jack Dalton Collection.)

A particularly memorable day was enjoyed by the Folkestone Corps on Tuesday, 1st August 1905 when the founder and leader of the Salvation Army, General William Booth, visited the town. He had arrived at Dover the previous morning on his return from visits to Australia and the Holy Land. The General was on the first stage of a motor car crusade which was to last a month and nine days and was aimed at encouraging his troops and to spark a new countrywide wave of religious enthusiasm.

The streets were packed and such was the enthusiasm shown by the townspeople of Folkestone that the General was one hour late arriving for his official reception by the Town Mayor, Alderman J. Banks, J.P., at the Pleasure Gardens Theatre. When General Booth walked on to the stage the audience, which included Edward and Elizabeth and the remainder of the Ramell family, accorded him a 'cordial demonstration.'

General Booth addressing the crowds on one of his many motorcades.
(Eileen Taylor Collection.)

The local newspapers gave a full account of the General's address making particular mention of his remark that the Salvation Army was held in high esteem all over the world. There was laughter when he added that, "it had not always been so, particularly in Folkestone!" - a reference to his knowledge of the 'Skeleton Army' activities there. The meeting finished with the Benediction and at 7 o'clock the General left the theatre escorted by four other motor vehicles and the Folkestone Corps Band playing from a charabanc drawn by four horses. It must have been a pleasing moment for Thomas Ramell playing before the General in a vehicle that he himself had manufactured.

Elizabeth and Edward's marriage was blessed on the 12th February 1906, with the birth of their only child, a daughter, Maisie Elizabeth Nye. Their happiness was short lived though as on the 20th November the same year, Maisie, at the age of just nine months, died at home of lobar pneumonia and convulsions.

Elizabeth and Edward oversaw the burial of their daughter on the 24th November at Folkestone Cemetery, Cheriton Road, Folkestone. She was buried in an unconsecrated part of the graveyard reserved for religions other than Church of England, in plot number 1113. Today there is no indication whether a gravestone was ever erected.

Postcard of the Folkestone Corps Band outside the Barracks in 1905.
Back Row: Second from right, George Meacher (See later chapters). Fifth from right, Thomas Ramell. Middle Row: Fifth from right, Edward Nye.
(Russell Lord Collection.)

A later outing for the Folkestone Corps Band, this time in a motorised charabanc.
(Alan F. Taylor Collection.)

'IN 1907 WE WENT TO CANADA'

It is likely that the death of little Maisie was the catalyst for the decision that Elizabeth and Edward subsequently made - to seek a fresh start in life in the New World. The Canadian Government was actively encouraging immigration at the time and had appointed a number of agencies, including the Salvation Army, as sponsors and paid grants for each immigrant's arrival.

To facilitate arrangements in the United Kingdom, a special Migration Department had been set up by the Army in London, in 1903. Nine soldiers from the Folkestone Corps, who would have been friends of Elizabeth and Edward, including Bandsman George Meacher, had preceded them to Toronto. No doubt encouraged by letters the nine had sent back home to their families, Elizabeth and Edward applied, and were accepted, for the crossing. They may well have studied the Salvation Army publication, *Emigration Gazette*, of 1907 which, long before anyone coined the phrase, 'politically correct', published an advertisement for The Canadian Pacific Railway Atlantic Steamship Lines, which listed amongst its Special Features, 'Good food, large cabins, no crowding. NO FOREIGNERS THIRD CLASS except Scandinavians'!

The Salvation Army International Heritage Centre Archives.

Cover of The War Cry, *22nd June 1907 reporting on one group of 1,000 emigrants leaving London for Canada.*

In June 1907, Elizabeth and Edward made their move to Ontario and took up appointments with the Toronto Temple Corps. No records survive today to indicate their employments but they would have taken part in an initiative that was pioneered in Toronto in 1908, that of 'salvage work'. Today we know it as recycling, and its success in those early trials heralded the start of the Salvation Army Thrift Shops.

In November 1909, Elizabeth and Edward crossed the border into the United States by railroad and relocated to the National Salvation Army Headquarters situated at 120-130 West 14th Street, New York City.

Postcard Copyright, Salvation Army
(Inc) 1905.
(Author's Collection.)

The Carolus Building,
29 Charles Street NYC.
(Photographed in Nov 2001 by Debbie Danson.)

It was here that Elizabeth took up employment in the tailoring department and Edward applied to join the band and became the Janitor/Night Watchman.

The couple took lodgings at the Carolus Building, 29 Charles Street, just a few blocks away from the Headquarters building.

Elizabeth Nye, wearing the style of uniform she became adept at making in the Tailoring Department.
(Salvation Army National HQ Archives and Research Center, USA.)

The Central Provincial Commander in New York at this time was Colonel William A. McIntyre. He had been specifically appointed to deal with the growing menace of drunkenness in the City and he controlled the Army's efforts to win those addicted over to God. One particular experiment he devised was his 'Boozers' Convention', which started on

Thanksgiving Day 1910. It was to be an all-out attack on 'Bums Row' in New York City.

Posters reading, 'Free Eats All Day', were posted on lampposts and billboards in all the worst affected areas. From early morning, Salvation Army personnel scoured the backstreets in buses and picked up all the sorrowful drunkards they could find. They were then transported to Memorial Hall where they were fed, and the errors of their ways were pointed out to them.

In the afternoon, a 'Boozers Parade' was held in which the entire force of the New York Salvation Army took part. The parade consisted of several brass bands, a waterwagon, floats depicting scenes in the life of a drunkard and, most striking of all, a 'Walking Whiskey Bottle', ten feet high, to which was chained a reeling, bloated drunk, followed by a shawled poverty-stricken woman and her ragged children. Many converts were made and the event proved so successful that it was carried on for a number of years. The Folkestone couple were learning that things were done with a great deal more panache in America than they had ever experienced at home!

'Boozers' Day Parade' in New York City.
(Salvation Army National HQ Archives and Research Center USA.)

The hopes that Elizabeth must have harboured of a new, settled and contented life were to be cruelly dashed however on 20th May 1911 when, just a week prior to her 29th birthday, Edward was admitted to the New York Hospital suffering from chronic endocarditis. He died two days later. Edward was buried at Kensico Cemetery, Valhalla, 40 miles north of New

York City. There he shares a common grave with two other fallen comrades. Elizabeth went to stay with Salvation Army colleagues in East Orange, New Jersey.

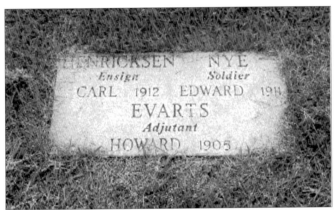

Grave marker for Edward Nye, at Kensico Cemetery.
(Photograph by Brian Meister.)

In an effort to come to terms with the loss of her husband, Elizabeth returned to England shortly after his death to be with her family for a long period of convalescence. It was her intention, at that time, to remain permanently in Folkestone.

During this period at home Elizabeth's parents gave her a copy of The National Comprehensive Family Bible. The opening page describes it as, 'The Holy Bible with the commentaries of Scott and Henry, and containing

Elizabeth's copy of The National Comprehensive Family Bible.
(Author's Collection.)

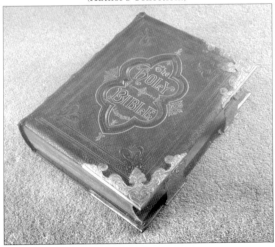

also many thousand Critical and Explanatory Notes selected from the Great Standard Authors of Europe and America. The Commentaries condensed and the whole edited by the late Rev John Eadie, D.D., LL.D Professor of Biblical Literature to the United Presbyterian Church. With a series of high-class coloured plates from original paintings by F. Goodall, R.A., P.R. Morris, A.R.A. and Miss Gow, and numerous litho.

'Transfers of steel plates from pictures by Eminent Masters, Coloured Maps, Family Register and Portrait Album.'

(Author's Collection.)

It must have been with a very heavy heart, and many tears, that Elizabeth herself wrote in the Family Register Section her own, and Edward's birth dates, their marriage details, and then recorded the death of both her husband and her daughter.

RECALL TO NEW YORK

Elizabeth had made many friends during the eighteen months she had spent at the New York Headquarters and her work in the tailoring department had been highly regarded. Following a personal request from the USA Commander, Evangeline Booth, daughter of General William Booth, Elizabeth was persuaded that she should resume her career in America.

General William Booth with Evangeline.
(Author's Collection.)

Through the Salvation Army migration department Elizabeth booked, for ten guineas (£10.50), a sailing for the first week in April 1912 on the Leyland Liner, *S.S. Philadelphia.*

A strike by coal miners had begun in Britain at the end of February over the Miners Federation 'Crown and Florin' demand, that the private owners of all of the country's coalmines should pay adult underground workers a minimum of five shillings (25p) a day, and two shillings (10p) for boys. The strike was to prove the direct cause of Elizabeth's involvement in the next tragic episode of her life.

The Liberal Government of the day supported the miners but found itself powerless to compel the owners to capitulate. The dispute dragged on and was only resolved when the Government passed the Coal Strike Act, which agreed in principle with a minimum wage but did not go so far as to state the amounts. A ballot of the striking miners took place and the strike was declared over on the 6th April.

By this time coal reserves around the country, particularly those for train travel and shipping, were severely depleted and a number of fuel conservation measures were in effect. The White Star liner *S.S. Olympic*, had sailed from Southampton on the 3rd April under instructions to husband her coal stock by not steaming any faster than 20 knots on her transatlantic voyage to New York.

The White Star Line was about to put a new liner into service. Not willing to allow the shortage of coal to jeopardise the maiden voyage of their new, luxurious liner, they made arrangements to transfer the coals, and passengers from a number of other liners, including the *Philadelphia*, across to their 'practically unsinkable' liner. Thus it was that Elizabeth Nye, at the age of 29, found herself embarking for America aboard the pride of The White Star Line, *R.M.S. Titanic*.

The White Star Line Passenger Liner, Titanic, *1912.*
(Author's Collection.)

Elizabeth Nye.
A pastel sketch by Penny Bearman.
(Author's Collection.)

'I WAS PLACED VERY COMFORTABLY IN A SECOND CLASS CABIN'

On Tuesday, 9th April 1912, having made a farewell visit to the grave of little Maisie, and completed her packing, Elizabeth travelled to Southampton in readiness to board the *Titanic* the following morning. She had decided not to take the Family Bible to America with her, presumably because of its weight of nearly 6 kilos. It was a decision that was to save the gift from certain slow destruction beneath the Atlantic. *1*

Elizabeth was accompanied on the train journey to Southampton by her sister Beatrice and the two women had stayed overnight with Salvation Army friends in the town. They arrived at the docks the following morning with time to spare so they went for refreshments. Elizabeth, already a veteran of two Trans-Atlantic voyages in smaller vessels, expressed concerns at travelling on a ship the sheer size of the *Titanic*. Beatrice berated her older sister using their childhood taunt, "You silly cat! That's the *Titanic*, she's unsinkable!" Elizabeth relented and boarded the ship whilst Beatrice wished her Bon Voyage.

On board the *Titanic,* Elizabeth shared Second Class cabin 33 on F Deck, with Miss Amelia Mary Brown (16), a cook employed by the Allison family (who were travelling first-class), of 152 Abbey Road, West Hampstead, London NW (the same road which was to later feature on the

Elizabeth, circa 1911. The War Cry (UK), 4th May 1912.
(Salvation Army International Heritage Centre Archives.)

cover of the Beatles 1969 album of the same name), Mrs Amelia Lemore (34), a British lady who was married to an American. She had been living in Camberwell, Surrey and was now returning to Chicago, and Mrs Selena Cook (22), 52 Grosvenor Street, West London, whose ticket had been booked in her maiden name of Rogers, who was travelling to Greenwich, Connecticut to visit her widowed mother.

The *Titanic* departed from Berth 44 promptly at midday assisted by six tugs. As she entered the channel of the River Test under her own power the vast wash given out by the giant liner caused the lines which had been tying the American Lines liner *S.S. New York,* alongside the White Star Lines *S.S. Oceanic*, to snap. Both ships had been idled by the coal strike. The *New York* started to drift towards the *Titanic* and a collision between the two seemed inevitable. Rapid action taken by the Captain of the tugboat *Vulcan* and Captain Smith of the *Titanic,* miraculously prevented the impending crash.

The *Titanic* continued her voyage and made a stop that evening at Cherbourg on the northern coast of France. Queenstown on the west coast of Ireland was reached the following day, where more passengers and mail were collected. She then set off heading west for New York with her passengers looking forward to a pleasant five day crossing without further incident.

Elizabeth later recalled that it became very cold on the evening of Sunday, 14th April. She joined a number of other second class passengers who had gathered together in their dining room for a Church of England Service. It was conducted by the Reverend Carter and there was a choir composed of twenty stewards. During the service the Reverend announced that this was the first time that hymns had been sung aboard the *Titanic* on a Sunday evening, and he hoped that it would not be the last. The service ended with the hymn, '*Oh hear us when we cry to Thee, For those in peril on the sea.*'

When Elizabeth and her cabin companions retired to bed, the three male occupants of the neighbouring cabin could be heard engaging in a pillow fight and generally enjoying a jolly time. The ladies eventually drifted to sleep only to be awoken at about 2340 hrs when the *Titanic* collided with the iceberg. They discussed the noises they had heard which had sounded like a horrid grating sound of running into gravel and then a flush of water before the engines had stopped. They found no reason to be afraid. Mrs Lemore ventured onto the deck and upon her return the four ladies decided that they should all dress and go and investigate further. They did so and went on deck, more out of curiosity, it appears, than fear. It was a move that was to save the lives of all four.

'LADIES AND CHILDREN IN FIRST'

During the subsequent evacuation of the *Titanic,* Elizabeth was placed into lifeboat No 11, which was launched about 0125 hrs and carried a full complement of 65 persons. Earlier lifeboats had left the ship seriously undermanned due to difficulties in convincing passengers of the seriousness of the situation. That lifeboat 11 was fully loaded, indicated the realisation of how critical things had become. The lifeboat was crewed by two sailors and fourteen male Stewards under the command of Quartermaster Sidney James Humphreys.

A front page sketch of the final scene, drawn by Paul Theriat, for the French daily illustrated paper, Excelsior.

(Author's Collection.)

As the lifeboat reached the water, it started to drift towards the water pumps outlet that was gushing a heavy stream of water - a scene that has been portrayed in nearly every movie subsequently made about the *Titanic* disaster. Careful handling prevented the lifeboat from being swamped and the crew started to row away from the ship. The occupants of the lifeboat could hear the band playing on the *Titanic* as they moved from the stricken vessel.

When they were about a quarter of a mile from the *Titanic* the crew stopped rowing, save for keeping the boat up head to the wind, and awaited rescue. About 0220 hrs, a huge roar was heard from the *Titanic* and the awful plight of those who had remained aboard was realised by the survivors in the lifeboats who then saw the ship disappear beneath the surface. A number of women in lifeboat 11, became understandably half-hysterical with concern over their absent husbands and friends. Later there were complaints amongst some of the ladies in the boat that they were so crushed together they could not sit properly. Others were offended by the fact that a number of the seamen had smoked cigarettes during their ordeal.

It was in Elizabeth's lifeboat that First Class survivor, Edith Russell, a well-known stylist and importer, had with her a lucky mascot of a musical pig with which she kept the children amused. The pig, which played the tune, 'La Maxixe', had inadvertently been responsible for saving Miss Russell's life. In all the confusion she had been too scared to jump into the lifeboat and had only done so when someone threw the pig in first. Miss Russell found the novelty on the floor of the lifeboat and saw that its forelegs were broken. However, it still played and she was able to keep the children in the lifeboat contented with its music. [*2*]

Also in lifeboat 11 was a ten-month-old baby, Frank Phillip Aks, who had become separated from his 17-year old Russian mother, Leah. Some reports suggest that it was Elizabeth who cared for the child in the lifeboat before rescue came. [*3*]

No matter how desperate a situation, humour can sometimes proffer a brief distraction. One of the seamen in the lifeboat was heard to comment, "This is my third shipwreck. If I get out of this one I'm going home to be a milkman!"

Fortunately for the survivors the sea remained calm. There were many stars in the sky but the night was so black that the ice floes around them could only be seen when they came close. The night was also bitterly cold. Although lifeboat 11 was to spend about six and a half hours in the water, to many on board it seemed as if just one hour had elapsed before the lights of the rescue ship, the Cunard liner *S.S. Carpathia*, could be seen. As they drew closer to the ship they saw other lifeboats also making for her.

Once alongside, the babies were the first to be taken out of the lifeboat. They were hoisted up in canvas bags and then a boatswain's chair was lowered for the ladies. They were each told to sit on its wooden seat and then close their eyes and hang on very tightly for the transfer to the *Carpathia*.

Once aboard, Elizabeth found herself quartered with the same three fellow companions with whom she had shared her cabin on the *Titanic*. Space was of course at a premium on the smaller *Carpathia* and the four ladies were given straw beds with brown blankets to sleep on in an area near the steerage survivors. Elizabeth was one of the few people to possess a comb with her and this item was much in demand by the other ladies.

The following morning Elizabeth was one of the few survivors who found that the dreadful experience they had gone through, although it had shattered her nerves, had had no effect on her hunger and she went for breakfast. She spent the remainder of the day composing the letter back to her parents which she then handed in to the ship's Post Office where it was franked, 'Royal Mail, Steamship Carpathia, Tuesday April 16th'.

The *Carpathia*, which had been bound from New York to Gibraltar, altered course and headed back to New York to land the survivors. Its radio operator, Harold Cottam, helped by the surviving *Titanic* operator, Harold Bride, (another Kent resident - from Shortlands near Bromley), spent the next three days transmitting personal wireless messages and lists of the survivors.

Back in Folkestone, Elizabeth's parents, Thomas and Elizabeth, learned from the morning papers on Tuesday 16th April, that a disaster had befallen the ship on which their daughter had been travelling. The couple faced an agonising wait of 24 hours whilst just meagre facts of the catastrophe filtered through, before learning from the London newspaper editions that Elizabeth was listed amongst those saved. Their feelings were those of unspeakable relief. Thomas chose the medium of the *Folkestone Herald* to express his thanks to the many kind enquirers and sympathisers who had visited them during their trying time.

Prior to the arrival of the *Carpathia* in New York, the American immigration authorities had announced that normal immigration procedures would be waived in respect of the *Titanic* survivors. There would therefore be no requirement for the rescue ship to offload the steerage passengers first at Ellis Island. Fearing that the *Carpathia's* arrival at the Cunard Dock would cause the dock to be overrun with media and sightseers, the police organised a pass system to ensure that only the members of the relief agencies, the five hundred expected relatives of the survivors, and Cunard officials would be allowed access. Many thousands more people waited outside the dock, all eager to witness the arrivals. It was estimated that another 10,000 people had crowded at Battery Point, the first vantage point from which the *Carpathia* would be seen.

The *Carpathia* finally arrived at Pier 54 on the Thursday evening. Amongst the relief agencies present was a committee of five members of the New York Stock Exchange who carried with them $20,000 in small bills to be handed out to all survivors who were destitute. The Salvation Army was also represented having made their arrangements for the offer of spiritual relief, clothing and accommodation of the survivors. The Army had also offered its Headquarters as temporary accommodation for any steerage passengers who wished to remain for a while in New York.

The Salvation Army contingent was headed by Evangeline Booth and included a reporter for *The War Cry*, and Captain George Darby, a gifted musician who then held an appointment with the Men's Relief Department and was the Deputy Bandmaster of the National Staff Band. Other Salvation Army personnel distributed refreshments to all those in need.

Band Member George Darby, circa 1909.
(Ruth Freeman Collection.)

The Army were to take a number of survivors under their wing that evening including Elizabeth, who was greeted by her Commander with a kiss, and also Mrs Rosa Abbott, the only other Salvationist who had been a passenger on the *Titanic*. *4 *

The first report of the *Titanic* disaster to appear in the US editions of *The War Cry* was in the 4th May copy which, under the heading, 'Loss of the *Titanic*', gave a lengthy account of the facts as known at that time, and concluded with these paragraphs:

'Salvationists will be particularly interested in the loss of the Titanic, as it was the boat on which the Commander was to sail. Our leader is making the trip for the purpose of consulting with the General, the Chief of the Staff and leading International officers on important matters dealing with the Salvation War in this country. All being well, she will now sail on the Mauretania on Wednesday, April 24th, and will be accompanied by Colonel William Peart, Chief Secretary.

The Carpathia, which is bringing the survivors of the Titanic to port, will be remembered as the steamship that took the happy, joyous American contingent of Salvationists to the last International Congress.

Mr. W. T. Stead, who we are afraid is to be counted among the lost, was a well-known friend of the General, and of The Army, and an advocate of its principles. Let us unitedly pray that God will give solace to the hearts of the family of this good man, and of all others who perished in this fearfully sad disaster.

Mrs. Nye, who assisted in the dress-making room at National Headquarters, was a passenger on the Titanic. She is, we are glad to say, reported saved.'

The following somewhat dramatised report of the landing appeared in the next US edition of *The War Cry*;

Landing of the Titanic's Survivors

Heartrendering Scenes at the Cunard Dock.

The Cunard dock in New York between the hours of 9 and 12 p.m. on Thursday, April 18th, was the scene of the most profound human agony that the mind can possibly conceive. It was dumb, too deep for words in most cases; in some it found outlet in shrieks of plain human anguish that made the blood clot and curdle in the vein-channels.

Salvationists will remember the Carpathia as the good, smooth-sailing liner that took a ship-load of us to the last International Congress in London and landed us safe and sound at the port of destination; on the present occasion she was well described as a hospital-ship, for she contained the pitifully few hundreds of those who alone had escaped from the Titanic as she "made port," as one paper grimly put it, two miles beneath the ocean's surface - and they in such a fearful condition of mind and body as to have warranted the ship that housed them in flying the Red Cross banner at her mast-head.

Commander Miss Booth, attended by the Chief Secretary and some of the National Staff, armed with passes, successfully negotiated the police lines, and, crowding through the tens of thousands of anxious, excited people who crowded the sidewalks and blocked the roadways, was at the dock in good time, and as the white-faced refugees landed in small groups, unnerved and hysterical, our beloved leader, with her womanly tact and sympathy, with a pat on the cheek here and a kiss for a forlorn woman or child there, with words of deepest sympathy for all and offers of relief to many who sadly stood in need of it, the Commander did her very best, ministering angel that she is, to assuage the heart-agony of these thrice-pitiful fellow creatures.

One of the first sights that focused itself upon the eye of the War Cry man was a poor fellow that, first of all, we thought was demented and then possibly intoxicated. His conduct suggested this. He had been waiting patiently for news of his family; they were all lost, but in sympathy the distressing tidings were kept back; finally, he demanded to hear the worst, and when told he gave an unearthly yell, threw up his hands and thrashed the air, then reeled to and fro, finally bringing up against the dockside with a bang. On the suggestion of the Commander we approached him with a word of comfort, but he waved us away. A Catholic priest went to him on a similar mission, but to him also was turned a deaf ear. The poor fellow's face, in the intensity of his agony, turned a purplish red, while the veins stood out like whip-cords as he shouted at the top of his voice; "Go away! Oh, go away! I don't want to see anybody or speak to anybody for a month!" He was inconsolable.

The thin, solitary procession continued down the gangway. It was evident many of them had been buoying themselves with the hope that their relatives on the Titanic had been picked up by other passing boats, and when the sad truth was made known to them the look of hopelessness upon their pain-marked faces was indescribable.

Here comes Mrs Hanson, a Scandinavian; she is alone. Suggestive word that! For when Mrs Hanson left Denmark she was not alone - her husband and son were with her. They were bringing her to start life over again in free, opportunity-giving America. They were taken and she was left, and what could she do now? That, indeed, was a question beyond our power to answer.

A man from the third cabin comes ashore clad only in shirt, pants and shoes. But his life is saved, and he smiles as we mention it.

A Swede - broad and with the look of a farmer - tells us with a choke in his voice that he was in charge of a party of five. But they are all gone; he is the only one rescued. He does not state how he is so fortunate as to find port, and we have not the heart to inquire too minutely, but we wish the party of five were with him.

There follows next a thin-legged little laddie who bears a foreign name.

"And where are your parents, and brothers and sisters?"

"All lost! All under the water!"

The little man goes on to tell us that he made a flying leap to a lifeboat that was already overfull, but he landed safely and was allowed to remain. Here he is in America without a friend.

The toll of the dead is indeed a fearful one. We shall never know the complete story of the iceberg-ramming Titanic until the opening of the books on the last Great Day. In the meantime wives have been widowed, children rendered fatherless, families broken, some wiped out altogether. It is only fitting that the flags have been flying at half-mast for several days past.

MRS. NYE'S STORY

There were two Salvationists among the refugees - Mrs. Nye and Mrs. Abbott.

Mrs. Nye is the young widow of one of the Headquarters janitors who passed away last year. Mrs. Abbott is an old-country local officer who made up her mind to come to the Land of Promise. There were just these two lone women by themselves. Would to God there had been four saved instead of two, then we should not have had to chronicle the sad fact that Mrs. Abbott's two bright boys had to take their stand with the men on the doomed ship while the women were piled into the boats. Mrs. Abbott suffered frightfully from exposure - in fact, her poor body was frozen right up to the hips. She lies in a hospital-cot as we write, and with a pitiful attempt at a smile tells us of one of her bonnie boys helping put her in the boat and, with the spirit of a true Salvationist, being willing to sacrifice himself. Let us pray for our dear comrade, and pour out our sympathy upon her as we thank God for the bravery of her boys now in their last sleep upon the ocean's bed.

"Mrs. Nye was greeted with a woman-kiss from the

Commander. The sister has gone through the ordeal in a most wonderful way, and was good enough to give the War Cry a fairly connected story of the disaster as she witnessed it. First of all, though, she excused herself as she had left something on board and wanted to fetch it.

"What do you think it was she fetched from the Carpathia? Make a guess!

"A little yellow canary bird in a brass cage! That was the woman of it! The poor little chap was a little bedraggled; he had been through all the horrors of shipwreck, but not forgotten how to chirp. Mrs Nye had lost money, clothes - everything, but here was a little bit of life she thought should not be forfeited, and she had saved him.

"The good sister was in the very last lifeboat to leave the doomed ship. She said, in answer to our questioning:

"Yes I saw the Titanic go down to her grave. She was a splendid ship, as you know. She did not sink flatly, like boats sail the ocean, but tipped up on end, and when she was half- submerged she broke completely in two and the lights went out. Five minutes before the engines stopped and everybody abandoned hope.

"No, we were not a bit scared at first, with most of the others.

"I was in bed when she struck; we felt the shock, of course but did not fear. Somebody said to me, "It's just an iceberg." Knowing where we were, that did not seem much at first. But we were all curious to know what had really happened, so we threw on what clothes were handiest and made our way upstairs. Then it was fear took possession, for we saw them making preparations to lower the boats, and we were ordered to remain on deck.

"We could not go back for any of our belongings. There was very little confusion. The men on the whole behaved splendidly. The women and small

children were put in the boats. I got in the last that
was launched.

"The engines fell out with a terrible roar which I
shall never forget.

"We drifted for about five and a half hours. It was a
beautiful night, as clear as could be. The water was
perfectly smooth. It was just as dawn was breaking
that the Carpathia came alongside us and picked us
up.

"No other boat came in sight, so there was no
possibility of any further rescues.

"It was a quarter before eleven that the boat struck.
There was but one iceberg as far as I could see
although there were thirty miles of icefields all
around us. I saw the iceberg that sent the Titanic to
the bottom, it caught the ship on one side and ripped
her completely open.

"The cries for help were awful, and are still ringing
in my ears. A man jumped into one of the boats and
was shot at, but they missed him and he was saved.

"It was bitterly cold. Many of the people on the boats
were insufficiently clad, and the suffering from
exposure was not by any means small. In fact, on the
Carpathia there were seven burials, but whether all
of these died from exposure or not I do not know;
some of them did; possible others were bodies picked
up from the water; for there were many floating
about.

"One of the memories that will remain with me to
my dying day is that of the band playing the familiar
air, "Nearer My God To Thee", as the lights went
out and the Titanic went to the bottom.

"Several of the lifeboats capsized. Perhaps they were
in the zone of suction. I don't know. Twenty boats
were lowered but only fourteen survived. One boat
when picked up contained only a single boatman; in
another seven were lying dead.

"Rafts were lowered in addition to the lifeboats. There were thirty people on one, but the exposure was so great that they all perished one by one, and as they died the bodies were pushed off into the water so as to lighten the burden and give a better chance to those alive. One man swam around in the icy water for three and three-quarter hours. He was a steward and was finally rescued, more dead than alive.

"Of course, the Carpathia had a pretty full passenger list of its own and could not give us first-class accommodations, but they did the best they could and treated us splendidly, giving us hot coffee and cordials and attending to our needs very largely at the expense of their own passengers' comfort. It was very kind and good of them, I am sure."

Mrs Nye was taken in hand by Army comrades and piloted to a temporary home with a heart full of gratitude to God for her deliverance.

Just as we were about to leave the dock a piercing shriek rent the air. We turned round just in time to witness a most pathetic scene. It appears one of the rescued women had been vainly seeking her brother, whom she expected at the dock to meet her. He on his part had been vainly in search of his sister, and had almost given up hope when he caught sight of her and she of him simultaneously. She was soon weeping hysterically upon his shoulder, and we could somewhat gage the depth of the poor woman's anguish when she cried out, "O George, George I thought I should never see you again! O George, don't let them blame me for not saving the children! I tried to, but I couldn't!" She was the only one of the family group saved; the others - husband and children - were all drowned!

These were experiences that burnt themselves into the brain and made the heart quiver, and the night was full of them. The Commander's heart was cut to the quick, and the same can be said of the members of the party.

THE ARMY'S HELP

The Salvation Army, as ever, rendered every service in its power to lessen the suffering. As stated elsewhere, accommodation was offered at the No. 1 Industrial Home, the S.A. Hotel at Chatham Square, the Women's Rescue Home and the New York Training College. At the latter place, as we write, ten Scandinavian men and women are enjoying the Army's hospitality.

During the landing of the survivors, Army lasses served hot coffee and meat sandwiches to the helpers and to all refugees who cared to partake. In this matter, as well as caring for the survivors apportioned to The Army's charge, Major and Mrs Cowan are worthy of special mention.

This account of the disaster by *The War Cry* is at variance on a number of points with the later determined facts;

The actual time that the *Titanic* had struck the iceberg was 2340 hrs.

Lifeboat No 11, in which Elizabeth had been placed, left the ship about 0125 hrs, at which time there were still four more boats preparing to leave.

There is no record of any of the lifeboats capsizing and all 20 arrived safely at the *Carpathia*, none were lost.

Mention of 30 persons on a raft perishing is complete fiction, as is the suggestion that anyone could have survived for three and three-quarter hours swimming in the icy cold water.

A burial service was conducted aboard the *Carpathia* for four victims. One passenger who had died in a lifeboat and three *Titanic* crewmen who had succumbed to shock and exposure shortly after arriving on the rescue ship.

It seems likely that either Elizabeth was inaccurately quoted for the sake of journalistic licence, or, that she had made mention of a number of rumours that had been circulating between the survivors concerning items which she had not personally witnessed. Certainly it is a strange story that she managed to carry a caged canary through the terrible events of that night, and even stranger that she failed to make mention of this in the letter to her parents, or indeed any subsequent references to the disaster. For these reasons alone I am personally inclined to discount this particular story.

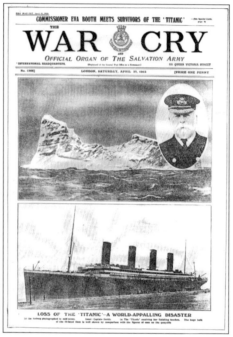

Cover page of The War Cry, *27th April 1912, UK Edition.*
(The Titanic Disaster was never featured on the cover of the US War Cry).
(Salvation Army International Heritage Centre Archives.)

The worst example of confused and inaccurate reporting regarding Elizabeth appeared, surprisingly, in a Salvation Army newspaper in the UK when, in its edition of 27th April 1912, *The Bandsman, Songster and Local Officer* published this article listing Elizabeth as one of those lost aboard the *Titanic*;

AMONG THE VICTIMS

Sister Mrs Nye, daughter of Bandsman Ramell, of Folkestone, was among the victims of the Titanic disaster. This comrade was on her way to New York to take up an appointment at The Army's Trade Department.

We understand that the father of Bandsman Strobel, of Poplar, was also among the drowned.

The paper was to publish a hasty retraction of this report in the following edition.

THE 'TITANIC' DISASTER

In a portion of last week's issue of the 'B.S.L.' it was erroneously stated that Sister Mrs Nye, daughter of Bandsman Ramell, of Folkestone, was one of the victims of the Titanic disaster. On the contrary, this comrade, we are glad to state, was rescued, and safely arrived in the Carpathia at New York, where she is employed in the Territorial Headquarters.

The following Bandsmen of Ballymacarrett were among the army of workmen employed at the building of Titanic: Bandmaster John Bell, moulder; Deputy-Bandmaster Geo. Nisbett, riveter; Bandsmen James Thompson, red-leader; Willie Nisbett, riveter; George Parker, mechanic; Samuel Lowery, blacksmith; Willie Burton, boilermaker; and James Aitken, french polisher.

A further inaccuracy involving Elizabeth can be found in the book 'The Sinking of the *Titanic* and Great Sea Disasters' edited by Logan Marshall. This was a hastily prepared account of the disaster and was compiled in 1912 in order to 'cash in' on the public's interest in the *Titanic*. It was sold for one dollar a copy by door-to-door salesmen across the United States. On page 150 Elizabeth Nye is mentioned as a survivor of the disaster, having been introduced two pages earlier as a member of the Salvation Army reception committee on the pier!

(Author's Collection).

The American and British National newspapers tended to reserve the majority of their coverage of the disaster for stories told by, or about, the high-profile passengers. Little coverage was given to non-public figures. The only mention of Elizabeth in a British National newspaper came in the *Daily Telegraph* of 25th April 1912 which stated, 'The War Cry this week publishes a cable from Commissioner Eva Booth at New York describing the measures taken by the Salvation Army in that city for relief of the *Titanic* survivors. Mrs Nye is the daughter of bandsman Ramell, of Folkestone, and is employed in the uniform department at New York. Those passengers were to have sailed on the *Philadelphia*, but, owing to dislocation in traffic, caused by the coal strike, that vessel's sailing was cancelled, and they were subsequently transferred to the *Titanic. The War Cry* also published a message of sympathy sent by General Booth, and President Taft's reply, "I thank you sincerely for your kind words of sympathy." '

Elizabeth gained one further Regional Newspaper mention, in the *Surrey Advertiser* of 20th April 1912 which read, 'Mrs Elizabeth Nye, one of the second class passengers saved in connection with the *Titanic* disaster, is a sister-in-law of Mr F. Nye, of Bagshot, one of the bell ringers of the Parish Church. Mrs Nye is a widow, and was returning to her home in America, after a short stay in England.'

As soon as word of the disaster had first reached New York, a committee, comprised of fifteen prominent Society ladies, formed to organise monetary relief for the survivors. The subsequent records of 'The Woman's Relief Committee to *Titanic* Survivors,' which lists all payments made out from the fund, indicate that during April 1912 three separate disbursements totalling $200.00 were made to Elizabeth Nye. It is also recorded that she required a minor hospital operation as a result of the exposure that she underwent during the ordeal.

A check carried out at the Liverpool Insurance office where claims made by the survivors of the *Titanic* are still kept, has revealed no trace of a claim ever having been submitted by Elizabeth Nye. Perhaps she considered that the monies she had received in the US were sufficient to compensate for her losses. The claims that were submitted against the White Star Line totalled US $16,000,000. When the Company finally settled four years after the disaster, the amount paid out totalled less than one-twenty-fifth of that claimed.

Similar fund raising events were taking place all over England to raise money for the relief of the survivors. In Folkestone, a hastily arranged parade of bands was held on Sunday, 28th April and it must have been with a heart full of happiness at his daughter's safe rescue that Thomas Ramell

A rare postcard of the Carpathia.
(Brian Ticehurst Collection.)

led the Salvation Army Band through the town. They were joined by the Hythe Fire Brigade Band and the Hythe Town Military Band on a march through the main streets which ended outside the Town Hall for a rendition of, *Nearer My God To Thee*. The newspaper reports stated that, 'The parade had attracted an immense crowd and practically every man had uncovered his head'. The procession raised the sum of £14 16 shillings and 1 penny - equivalent to over £500 in today's values.

As an aside to the *Carpathia* story, after the ship had landed the survivors and refuelled, the journey to Gibraltar was recommenced . During the voyage an inventory carried out by the victualling department revealed that over 200 *Carpathia* monogrammed spoons and forks had disappeared - presumably taken by many of the survivors as souvenirs.

Later in 1912, on Tuesday, 20th August, General Booth, then in his 83rd year and totally blind following an unsuccessful operation, was resting quietly at his home in Hadley Wood, North London. A telegram was delivered from Evangeline in New York. After being read out to him the message was put into his hand. As he was holding it he was 'Promoted to Glory' - a Salvation Army euphemism which is surely much more apt than the word, 'died.' The telegram read simply, "Give him a kiss for me."

General William Booth
(Author's Collection.)

The following day the General's will, written 22 years earlier, was read. In it he appointed his son and Chief of Staff, William Bramwell Booth, to succeed him.

'I'M GOING FORWARD TO DO GOD'S WILL'

Elizabeth resumed her career in the Tailoring Department and remained in contact with Captain Darby. Eventually romance was to blossom and the couple decided to marry. However, as marriage in the Salvation Army was not, at that time, permitted between a commissioned rank and a soldier, it was necessary for Elizabeth first to be commissioned herself. She applied for the training and the Candidates Personal Experience form she was obliged to complete read as follows;

Elizabeth Nye

Age: *Thirty-one years old*
Corps: *Harlem*
Date: *February 13th 1913*

My parents have been Salvationists in England since the year 1883, when the Army first opened up at Folkestone, Kent.

My father held the position of Bandmaster for twenty-one years, and since the year 1905 has held the position of Songster Leader etc.

I was converted while a junior, afterward took charge of a junior Sunday School class and later transferred to the Senior Corps.

In December of the year 1904, I was married to a Salvation Army bandsman.

In 1907, we went to Canada where we were soldiers of the Temple Corps of Toronto.

Later in 1909 we came to the National Headquarters New York and took up positions in the building. My husband died in New York Hospital on May 22, 1911.

God has called me for His work and I pray He will use me, and make a blessing in His service. My sins are all under the Blood, and I'm going forward to do God's Will.

Elizabeth began her training on the 13th October 1913 at the Officer Training College on Andrews Avenue and West Tremont Avenue, Bronx, New York.

Salvation Army College, Andrews Ave. and West Tremont Ave., Bronx, N. Y.
(Author's Collection)

Her course was successfully completed in April the following year and she was appointed a Probationary Captain in June 1914 and worked at the Boston Rescue Home for four months before moving on to the Philadelphia Home.

News of Elizabeth's impending marriage to George reached the media and the following article appeared in the New York Tribune on the 23rd May 1913;

OFF TITANIC, MET CUPID AT PIER

Elizabeth Nye to Wed Salvation Army Captain Whose Face She Saw First After Swoon on Landing Night - Girl Herself Becomes Worker in the Corps

A romance that began when the Carpathia landed the rescued Titanic passengers here will have its happy ending in a few weeks when Elizabeth Nye, a Titanic survivor, and now a cadet in the training college of the Salvation Army, becomes the wife of Captain George Darby, the Army's national headquarters staff bandmaster.

Captain Darby's face was the first the young woman saw when she opened her eyes after a swoon and found herself beside the pier in New York. Although hundreds of other persons of both sexes were in their immediate neighborhood, that first meeting, as far as they were concerned, settled the whole matter.

But, according to the laws of all romances, an obstacle to their marriage arose in a rule of the Salvation Army forbidding a union between a commissioned officer of the organization and one who is not identified with the movement.

This difficulty was soon overcome, however, by the young woman deciding to consecrate herself to the service of the Salvation Army. She will obtain her commission as a lieutenant in the Army on June 9.

"I would have devoted myself to work of the character I have determined to engage in any event," said the bride-to-be yesterday. "My terrible experience on the Titanic settled that question in my mind. There were four in my cabin. We were all saved through the mercy of God. For some years I had considered the question of volunteering my services to the Army, but held back on one pretext or another.

"Even before I entered the lifeboat on that terrible night I made a vow that I would give my life to the holy cause of lifting my fallen sisters up. That vow I would have kept under any circumstance."

Every effort has been made by the principals to keep their approaching marriage secret. But they admitted the engagement when someone at headquarters "gave them away."

Cadet Nye is one of the finest young women we have ever had in the college," said Colonel John Dean, principal of the school, last night. "She is alert, intelligent and devoted. She will make a splendid addition to our working force in the rescue department."

I suspect that the couple themselves would not have been best pleased at this article, the style of reporting of which promulgates their union as a love-at-first-sight romance, for the truth was a great deal more mundane. Clifford Greene was aware that the Ramell family had been friends with the Darby family in England for some time prior to any of them having emigrated across the Atlantic. Given both families interest in band matters it is hardly surprising that they would have met up often at Salvation Army Band events. Clifford produced from his photograph collection a picture, which may well have been taken in America by Elizabeth, which shows her first husband, Edward Nye, in an off duty moment together with George Darby.

George Darby and Edward Nye.
(Clifford Greene Collection.)

As both Elizabeth and George were also expatriates it is hardly surprising that this common bond meant that their friendship had continued after Elizabeth's return to New York. They must have also known that their lives up to that point had virtually mirrored each others.

George Darby had been born in Cannock, Staffordshire on the 23rd September 1883 into a Salvationist family who lived in a cottage on Rumer Hill, near Cannock. His father was a mining engineer and George had nine brothers and sisters. At the age of nine, George enlisted into the Salvation Army Cannock Corps where, for his marked musical ability at such a young age, he was granted the unusual honour of being drafted into the Senior Band. His rise within the band had been nothing short of meteoric and he was appointed Bandmaster whilst still in his teens. As a present, his parents bought him a euphonium and there was great excitement in the Darby household on the day that it was delivered in a wooden crate that was only just of a size to be passed through the cottage door. It seemed to take forever to be unpacked. George was so pleased with the instrument that he named it 'Rex'. Just like all the other instruments he chose to study, George became a master of its mellow tones.

George (right), and his father
James, leaving the cottage to attend
an Open Air Meeting in Cannock.
George is carrying 'Rex'.
(Ethel and Charles Edge Collection.)

Margaret Thompson Fraser
(Salvation Army International
Heritage Centre Archives.)

By 1901, at the age of 17 George was earning his living, along with two of his brothers, as a labourer at a local brickyard where their father was also employed as an engine driver.

On 28th August 1905, at the Wesleyan Methodist Chapel, Cannock, at the age of 21, George married Adjutant Margaret Thompson Fraser who was 13 years his senior and the daughter of a police constable.

The wedding was an unusual one as two of the couples' colleagues were also married at the same service. The marriages were reported in *The Advertiser* of Saturday, 2nd September, with the following article;

A SALVATION ARMY WEDDING

A double wedding was solemnised in the Wesleyan Church, on Monday afternoon, the contracting parties being Mr G. Darby, assistant master of the Salvation Army Band, and Miss Maggie Fraser. The second happy couple were Mr J. Nicholls and Miss Florence May Edwards. The bridegrooms are two soldiers belonging to the local corps of the Salvation Army, while the brides may, perhaps, be better known as Adjutant Fraser and Lieutenant Edwards, of Aberdeen and London respectively, and late officers in charge at Cannock. The church was crowded with people anxious to witness a Salvation Army wedding. The hymn, "O happy day," was sung, and then followed an appropriate prayer, offered by Colonel Whiller. A short ceremony followed, in which the usual vows were taken by the brides and bridegrooms. During the service Mr G. Darby played a euphonium solo. Mrs T. B. Angold kindly presided at the organ throughout the service, which was followed with keen interest.

Adjournment was made to the Barracks, which had been tastefully decorated for the occasion, and where a wedding banquet had been prepared. Over one hundred guests were in attendance. It may be mentioned that the bridegrooms and brides were attired in full army uniform, and those present included a number of army officials of various ranks, the brides' parents from Aberdeen and London, and relatives and friends from Brighton, Leicester, Birmingham, and other places. Adjutant Fraser and Lieutenant Edwards have been officers in the army for about fifteen years, and numerous letters and telegrams of congratulations were received during the day. The happy couples left by the 5.34 p.m. train for Blackpool, where the honeymoon is being spent.'

Margaret possessed a fine soprano voice. She was Scottish and had given her heart to God at the Aberdeen Citadel at the age of seventeen, at which time she had applied for, and been accepted for, officer training. Despite the opposition of friends she had entered the Fenny Stratford Depot as a Cadet but after a short time her precarious health had given way and she was advised to return home. Her determination to carry on, however, restored her health and she was soon serving as a Lieutenant at Sandown. At her next appointment, in Potton, she faced great opposition from 'the Skeletons' and in one attack her arm was broken.

At Southsea she was responsible for opening a new Citadel and two hundred souls were converted there. So concerned was she about these converts that she would get up early in the morning and pray with them before they went to work.

Margaret was later promoted to Captain and farewelled to a number of other appointments in the Midlands. At Salford, she delighted in visiting the poor and degraded. It was no unusual sight to see drunken women put their arms around her neck, while she was talking, and kiss her - so much had she won their hearts.

At her next appointment, in Wombwell, her health failed again, but so great was her love for her work that she had to be carried home after one Sunday night meeting.

At Leeds she was promoted to Ensign and at Dudley she succeeded in clearing off a debt of £150. Margaret was promoted Adjutant upon her move to Cannock where she met Bandmaster George Darby. There is little doubt that both George's and Margaret's love of music had been the initial reason they had been drawn together. Their marriage meant that, under Salvation Army rules, Margaret had to drop in rank to the equivalent of George's rank as Bandmaster, that of a Local Officer. The couple looked forward to the birth of their first child. It was not to be however, as on the 26th June 1907, Margaret and the child died due to complications brought about by the advanced stage of her pregnancy. Her funeral was reported in *The Advertiser* of 6th July.

SALVATION ARMY OFFICER'S DEATH

An Impressive Funeral

The very large crowd which attended the obsequies of the late Mrs G. Darby, who for many years was a well-known Salvation Army Officer, was actuated by more than mere curiosity, and was intended to show the respect and esteem in which the deceased was held, as well as being a sign of sympathy with the husband in the some-what tragical circumstances under which the bereavement occurred.

The funeral took place on Sunday, when the bandsmen assembled opposite the late home of the deceased officer. The coffin, covered with wreaths, having been placed on chairs, the hymn "Rock of Ages" was impressively sung, the band accompanying. Prayer was offered by Adjutant Dairymaple, and after a few appropriate words from Staff-Capt. Lewis, a procession was formed, and to the strains of, "Promoted to Glory", the cortege slowly wended its mournful way to the Salvation Army Hall, which was quickly packed with people. Several hymns were sung, and a solo, "Heaven," composed by deceased's husband, was rendered by Mr W. Field. An address was given by Mrs Winton, who alluded in fitting terms to the good life and work of Mrs Darby. Staff-Capt. Lewis read the lesson and conducted the service. The procession was re-formed, and proceeded to the cemetery, where the band, as the gates were reached, made themselves as a body-guard to the coffin, and in this order proceeded to the grave, where a brief service was conducted by Staff-Capt. Lewis. After the interment the band returned playing a lively march, the latter being in accordance with the wishes of the deceased. The cemetery was attended by at least one thousand people.

The mourners were Mr G. Darby (husband), Mr and Mrs James Fraser, sen., Scotland, Mr and Mrs James Fraser, Lizzie and Ella (sisters), Mr and Mrs and Miss Darby, and Mr Nicholls. The funeral arrangements were made by Mr Sellman.

In the evening the Army Hall was packed, when a funeral service was conducted by Staff-Capt. Lewis. Mr R. Beaumont, who delivered the address, said that the attendance that day showed the esteem and respect in which their departed sister was held by all around. She was a most successful officer, and probably her labours in the field might have shortened her life, but he thought her relatives would have the gratification of knowing that her life had not been spent in vain, for numbers had been influenced for good by her.

The cause of death was a tumour of ten years' standing, but which, owing to the strain and worry of Army work, had not developed. Since deceased

left the Army work and settled down to a less
strenuous life the tumour had assumed abnormal
proportions, thus displacing other organs of the
body, which ultimately caused unconsciousness and
death.'

George went into the depths of despair. He moved back to his parents'
home and would sit at the piano for such long periods picking out with one
finger the tune to Herbert Booth's composition, *With My Heart So Full Of
Sadness* that his family genuinely feared for his sanity. He eventually
started to come to terms with his loss but he needed the challenge that
could only be provided by new surroundings. He chose to emigrate to the
United States.

Prior to his departure George was presented, at a crowded gathering of
Salvationists, with a farewell gift of a standard-sized copy of The Holy
Bible, Collins Teachers Edition. Strangely enough, George also decided
against taking the gift with him and it remained in the UK. It is now owned
by Len and Doreen Williams, Darby family descendants. The Bible
inscription reads:

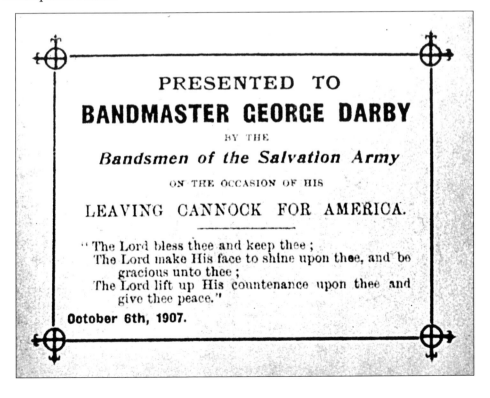

PRESENTED TO
BANDMASTER GEORGE DARBY
BY THE
Bandsmen of the Salvation Army
ON THE OCCASION OF HIS

LEAVING CANNOCK FOR AMERICA.

"The Lord bless thee and keep thee ;
The Lord make His face to shine upon thee, and be
gracious unto thee ;
The Lord lift up His countenance upon thee and
give thee peace."

October 6th, 1907.

George boarded the American Lines *S.S. Westernland* at Liverpool and arrived in Philadelphia later the same month. From there he travelled, by prior arrangement, to stay with an aunt in Fall River, Massachusetts. There he joined the local Salvation Army Corps and his remarkable musical ability was quickly appreciated and he was appointed Bandmaster. George's next move was to apply for a commission in order to gain a position with the National Staff Band who were based in New York City.

George was to write "I feel it my duty, being alone, to give my whole life to the Army and my *real* Father's Kingdom, knowing this is the only real joy, that can comfort me in my loneliness."

After passing through Training College in 1908 George was appointed a Probationary Lieutenant with the Eastern Social Service Department and later the Express Department in New York prior to his promotion to Captain in July 1909.

Postcard of the National Staff Band 1909, under Bandmaster
Robert Griffith, just prior to a tour of Canada.
Lt George Darby, middle row, extreme right.
(Author's Collection.)

George's qualities as an excellent musician and a born leader were recognised by Evangeline Booth and she put him in charge of the choirs at her 'Living Tableau' demonstration at Carnegie Hall. He was then appointed Acting Deputy-Bandmaster under Robert Griffith.

George had taken his euphonium, 'Rex', with him to the USA but one day, whilst he was purchasing a ticket at Pennsylvania Railroad Station in New York City, his dear trusted friend had been stolen. George vowed from then on to cease being a member of the band and to become its leader and conductor. Perhaps his reasoning was that all that could then be stolen from him was a baton! Thereafter, on occasions when the band would be on a motorcade with Evangeline Booth, if they passed a dump and saw someone poking through the rubbish, George would be teased with, "Oh look, there's George looking for his euphonium!"

Further appointments with the Eastern Social Statistical Department and the Reliance Book Store were carried out by George before he arrived at the Mens Relief Agency. All these duties were undertaken in addition to his band commitments and in 1912 he achieved his goal of being appointed Bandmaster of The National Staff Band, the position he held the night he was on Pier 54 to meet the Titanic survivors.

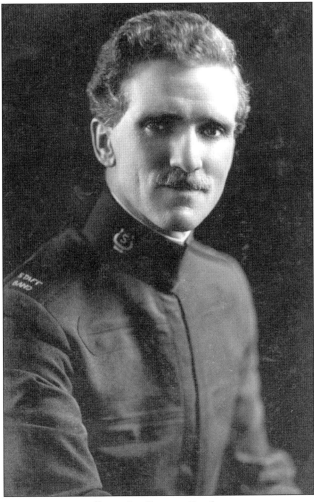

Captain George Darby.
(Ruth E. Freeman Collection.)

Elizabeth - deep in study.
(Jerilyn Sunlin Collection.)

'WE WILL RECEIVE OUR CANADIAN COMRADES STANDING'

Elizabeth Nye and George Darby married on the 26th November 1913 at the Salvation Army Chapel, 533 West 48th Street, the service being performed by Colonel William Peart. Invitations to the wedding were sent to a number of relatives in both families in England but it is thought that none were able to make the long and expensive journey across the Atlantic.

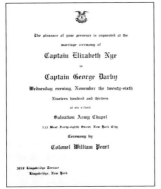

The Wedding Invitation.
(Clifford Greene Collection.)

Elizabeth and George set up home initially at 3019 Kingsbridge Terrace, Kingsbridge, a three-story apartment building on the West Side of the Bronx, just a short distance from the Harlem River.

The Darbys were to spend the rest of their careers without moving from the Headquarters in New York which was exceptional for Salvation Army Officers who are normally farewelled to a number of different Commands during their service. George excelled in his leadership of the National Staff Band and his musical skills combined with his teaching ability were to keep him in that appointment for a total of 19 years, a tenure of office that has not been equalled since.

Elizabeth was a tireless worker for the League of Mercy, a visitation programme that connects the Army with those with special needs in hospitals, nursing homes and correctional facilities. Those visited are taken books, sweets and most importantly a kind word or a shared prayer at every bedside. Many who are alone at Christmas receive gifts and Bibles. God's word, combined with the volunteer's caring lets the people know that they are never truly alone. Much of Elizabeth's work was carried out at Fordham Hospital, a short distance

The newly-weds pose in the garden of their NY home.
(Ron Vertone/Titanic Historical Society Collection.)

from the couple's home. She also frequently addressed meetings of the Women's Home League, groups of women of differing ages who would be spoken to on subjects such as hygiene, childcare or domestic matters. As one Salvationist to whom I spoke described it, "The Home League is the Women's Institute with hats!"

In June 1914, Elizabeth and George were part of a 700 strong delegation from the United States to the Grand International Congress held at the Crystal Palace in London, attended by delegates from every country in which the Salvation Army was represented. On the evening prior to their departure, Friday, 29th May, a special service was held at the New York Memorial Hall during which Captain Darby led the National Staff Band in a beautiful rendition of, *It Is Well With My Soul*. The enthusiasm held by the delegates for the forthcoming Congress was tempered by news from Canada of the disaster which that morning had befallen the Canadian Pacific liner *S.S. Empress of Ireland*. Whilst steaming along the St Lawrence River the liner, carrying 1477 passengers and crew, was struck by the Norwegian collier Storstad and sank within a 14 minute period. There were only 465 survivors. Of the 171 Canadian Salvationists who had also been on their way to the Congress on board the *Empress of Ireland* only 21 survived. Those lost included Commissioner and Mrs David Rees, Colonel and Mrs Maidment, many of the Territorial Headquarters staff and all but nine members of the Canadian Staff Band.

Commemorative postcard of the Empress of Ireland.
(Author's Collection.)

The War Cry reported that in New York the next morning, '*the parade to the White Star dock was a very picturesque and creditable sight. 700 military-garbed men and women marching to band music under the flags of the Army and the Nation was an inspiring spectacle. The crimson felt hats, the gray dresses of the women, and the "nifty" epaulettes of both men and women, the quaintly garbed young people's brigade, the brass band music, the two rows of color-bearers at the front, following the police guard, woke up the people of little old New York town on this Memorable Day. People wondered what had struck the city*'.

Back in Folkestone there was great consternation at the news of the *Empress of Ireland* tragedy, for one of those lost was George Meacher, the former member of Thomas' band who had emigrated to Canada prior to Elizabeth. A subsequent article appeared in the 6th June edition of the *Folkestone, Hythe, Sandgate and Cheriton Herald*. Beneath a photograph of the lost bandsman it read:

THE LATE MR G. MEACHER

Mr George Meacher, a son of Mrs Meacher who formerly carried on a business in the High-street was drowned in the Empress of Ireland tragedy. Mr Meacher, who was born in Folkestone, was in the Salvation Army Band, being for many years under the tutorship of Mr Thomas Ramell, the late bandmaster. He was a very fine cornet player and very popular amongst local Salvationists of this town. About ten years ago he married Miss May, and they went to Canada. He lived in Toronto and joined the Toronto Salvation Army Band. There was one child by the marriage, a daughter, now almost eight years old. He sailed with many other members of the Salvation Army from Canada who were coming to England to take part in the International S.A. Conference. His wife and daughter remained behind in Toronto, where the deceased was much esteemed. Mrs Meacher snr., who went to Canada after giving up the shop in High-street returned to Folkestone last Saturday. The late Mr Meacher, who was about 31 years old, was for some years an employee of Messrs. A. Stace and Sons, printers.

TRAVELLERS BY A LATER BOAT

Mr T. Ramell of Dover-road had a very anxious time when he heard of the sinking of the Empress of Ireland. His daughter, Mrs Darby, wife of the Bandmaster of a Salvation Army Band, had intended to travel by the ill-fated boat, but fortunately, she did not leave until Saturday last on the Olympic, sister ship to the Titanic. On Tuesday morning Mr Ramell received a letter from his daughter, saying that she was on the Olympic, and would be reaching Southampton about the 5th or 6th of June. It will be remembered that Mrs Darby (then Mrs Nye) was on the Titanic but was picked up by the Carpathia after being in an open boat for five hours. Mrs Darby has had a full share of trouble. Her first sweetheart was drowned in the Folkestone Harbour, and she was not married long before her husband, Mr Nye, died in a Newport Hospital. She also lost her two children, and she herself nearly succumbed to a very severe attack of appendicitis. She was married again last November. Mr T. Ramell wishes to thank all those who have made inquiries concerning his daughter.

A reasonably accurate report, albeit Newport instead of New York, and official records, confirm the loss of one child only. *The Folkestone Express, Sandgate, Shorncliffe and Hythe Advertiser*, in their report on the loss of the Empress also erred;

'Many have been the rumours concerning Mrs Nye, who was one of the survivors from the Titanic. Amongst other statements about her was that she was on the Empress of Ireland, and another was that she intended crossing by the vessel but was prevented from doing so at the last moment. We are assured by her father (Mr Ramell) that there is not the slightest foundation for any of the statements, but that she is safe in Montreal, where she resides with her husband, whom she married about four months ago. The local corps of the Salvation Army

> are holding a memorial service in the Bradstone
> Hall on Sunday evening at 6-30.

The US Delegation, and a number of Canadian Delegates who had chosen to travel with them, crossed on *S.S. Olympic*, sister ship to the Titanic. This must have caused many unpleasant memories for Elizabeth. She was pleased however, during the voyage, to meet up again with one of the stewards who had also been rescued from the *Titanic*, in the same lifeboat. From him she learned for the first time that their lifeboat had been number 11.

To while away the journey, prayer meetings were conducted and the bands aboard gave many concerts. Sporting events were also organised and a *War Cry* correspondent travelling with the group was later to write, 'In a tug-of-war on the *Olympic* eight of the largest men on board were pitted against eight Salvationists. The Salvationists were considerably outclassed in weight, but they pulled their opponents both ways easily. The ship's doctor was asked for an explanation, and he replied, "You never see these men with cigars or cigarettes in their mouths, nor drinking at the bar."

With Elizabeth and George's status as officers they may also have socialised with US ex-President Theodore Roosevelt who was a fellow passenger on the voyage and who agreed one afternoon to pose for a group photograph with the 200 Officers who were making the trip.

Ex-President Roosevelt with the Officers. Elizabeth and George are in there somewhere!
(Salvation Army National HQ Archives and Research Center USA.)

The ex-President also attended daily band rehearsals and his presence and broad smile of approbation were said to have given the men the inspiration to reach and maintain peak performance.

Back in the United States, the June 27th edition of *The War Cry* featured a collage of photographs taken on board the *Olympic* on its front page. Included was a picture of the New York Band being conducted by George Darby during a rehearsal on the upper deck of the ship.

The *Olympic* arrived at Southampton some days prior to the official start of the Congress on June 11th. It is likely that Elizabeth then travelled directly to Folkestone in order to visit her family as Thomas Ramell's health had been giving cause for some concern. George was obliged to remain in London with the Staff Band for whom three days of concerts and meetings at the Wood Green Citadel had been arranged.

The National Staff Band
Bandmaster George Darby seated fourth from right.
(Salvation Army National HQ Archives and Research Center USA.)

The Welcoming Meeting of the Congress was held at the Royal Albert Hall and there was a poignant moment for the delegates, particularly Elizabeth, when General Bramwell Booth instructed, "We will receive our Canadian comrades standing." The much depleted delegation plus two

'Congress of the Nations', 1914 programme.
(Author's Collection.)

survivors from the recent tragedy then quietly and bravely entered the Hall and took their places beside several rows of empty chairs, each of which had been draped with a white sash.

There followed a series of rallies and meetings at various locations throughout London. One afternoon had been set aside for a special event - the Officers of the American Delegation were invited on the 16th June to a reception at the American Embassy. The Officers assembled together with three bands at the Houses of Parliament and marched to the Embassy which was then situated in Victoria Street. There they were entertained by the American Ambassador, the Hon. Walter H. Page.

During a music festival held at the Royal Albert Hall, the National Staff Band surprised their audience by putting down their instruments to become a male voice choir. Under George's direction they sang his own choral composition, 'Wonderful.'

On Tuesday, 23rd June the Congress held a large event at the Crystal Palace, South East London. The programme indicates that the New York Staff Band were kept busy throughout the day and evening giving spaced concerts at a number of different events. What short time Elizabeth and George would have had together that day would have been enjoyed greeting their friends from the Folkestone and Cannock Corps who were also attending.

The International Congress had been held to mark the start of the Salvation Army's fiftieth year and a special commemorative medal was awarded to all attendees. The Congress was hailed as a great success. For many the highlight was the closing march held through the streets of London from Victoria Embankment to Hyde Park. Each delegation wore the traditional clothing of their country which all added to the atmosphere of a grand fancy-dress parade. The US contingent looked particularly resplendent with their uniforms topped with red stetsons. Evangeline Booth, who had always loved a display of costumes and pageantry, rode a fine black horse in front of George leading his Staff Band, one of 57 taking part in the parade.

The length of the entire parade can be judged from the one hour and forty minutes that it took to pass the reviewing stand. The US portion of the parade included a chuck wagon drawn by four horses flanked by Cowboy and Indian outriders. There was even a Salvationist dressed in the uniform of a prisoner at the infamous Sing Sing Prison. For Londoners, whose only experience of the Wild West was reading about it in adventure books, the parade must have presented a spectacular sight. *The Times* was to declare Evangeline Booth as the outstanding woman of the Congress and to describe her oratory skills as, 'the Old General come to life.'

The visit of the American Delegation to the Congress was recorded for posterity by an unknown member of the group who had taken along a 35mm kinetograph - a moving picture camera. The resultant 15 minute black and white silent film, which is now stored by the National Archives and Records Administration in Washington, DC., is a fascinating chronicle of the trip and portrait of the era. It opens with the caption, 'Delegates from every land attend a great international congress in London' and shows the moment of departure of the *Olympic* from the White Star Dock. The decks are thronged with uniformed Salvationists all waving their goodbyes. A large Blood-and-Fire flag was proudly flown at the ship's bow. There follows a view of the *Olympic* leaving New York Harbour.

The next footage, taken after arrival in London, shows groups of delegates from Sweden, Java, India, South America and South Africa. The latter group included adherents from Zululand in full ceremonial dress who had accompanied their colonial Salvation Army Officers to the Congress. The Zulus are seen breaking into a tribal war dance during which their Officers enthusiastically join in!

The film continues with General and Mrs Bramwell Booth on the reviewing stand at the Crystal Palace Celebration and shows Commissioner Lawley and other prominent Salvationist leaders.

The last portion of the film shows the Grand Parade of 50,000 Salvationists through the streets of London and was taken from an elevated advantage point along Oxford Street. The arrival of the American contingent is heralded by a figure dressed as Uncle Sam, who precedes a flag-bearing party carrying the Stars and Stripes and the various US Territory Salvationists flags. Evangeline Booth and Colonel Peart, the Chief Secretary (who had conducted Elizabeth and George's wedding the previous year), then come into view on horseback. They are followed by Captain Darby and the National Staff Band although the camera was too far away to allow any particular individual in a large group to be positively identified. Behind them marched a large group of Salvationist ladies which would have included Elizabeth. The ladies also wore the red stetsons with their long dresses and they waved white bandannas at the crowds who lined the streets. Newspaper estimates put the crowd at half a million.

Next to appear was the Worcester Band followed by a tableau of life in America. There was then another large contingent of representatives from the Eastern States. The third band in the American section was the Chicago Band which, in marked contrast to the National Staff Band, had a number of female musicians within its ranks. They were followed by an impressive tableau entitled, 'The World in America' - a large coach pulled by four horses on which American immigrants of many origins were seated in their former national costumes beneath a large globe highlighting the United States.

Shortly thereafter the film ends just as the Flint Band were coming into view. It is known that they in turn were followed by the representatives of the Western States with their Wild West theme. It is highly noticeable during the film that the gentlemen were continually doffing their hats and boaters to the ladies that they encountered. In all, the film gives a pleasing glimpse of a bygone age. Further glimpses can be seen in the photographs overleaf - also taken by a member of the American Delegation.

On June 28th, shortly after the Congress had finished, events in the Balkans were to cast a deep shadow over Europe. In Sarajavo two shots fired from a Browning automatic pistol by a 19 year old youth, killed the heir to the Austro-Hungarian throne, Archduke Ferdinand of Austria. This act started a chain of aggression that led to Germany attacking France by marching through, and violating the neutrality of, Belgium.

On completion of the Congress the delegates were free to visit with family and friends around Europe. Elizabeth and George made the one

A band rehearsal on SS Olympic.

A relaxing game of deck quiots.

A view from within the crowd of Ex-President Roosevelt.

In London, a visit to the grave of General William Booth at Abbey Park Cemetery, Stoke Newington.

The 'World in America' float.

The Wild West comes to London.

hour and forty minute train journey south to Folkestone. Thomas' health had been failing further and this was to be the last opportunity Elizabeth had to see him alive. Elizabeth and George returned to New York just prior to the British declaration of war with Germany, on August 4th.

Under George's leadership, the reputation of the National Staff Band was steadily increasing and the 35 musicians found themselves playing at more prestigious events than ever before. George had a vision for the finest sacred music and he held this up as a goal for his bandsmen. He was to explain his theory of Salvation Army music in the following article written during the early years of his tenure as Bandmaster:

'*Far more than any other religious body of people can it be said of The Salvation Army that we have a musical and singing religion. It was this that attracted me in my very early boyhood. I firmly believe that a great measure of the success of The Salvation Army has been brought about by its music.*

Many Salvation Army bandsmen approach their music in the wrong spirit; they lack the deep reverence and worshipful attitude that is absolutely necessary. To some it is purely a selfish pleasure, and to others an opportunity to show off their ability.

Any success that has come to me personally I credit to the fact that as a young boy I recognised the sacredness of my calling. To me my music has always been just as much a service for Christ as any other part of a Salvation Army meeting. So deep was this feeling impressed upon my heart that I never once took my instrument to practice, or began my studies, without first closeting myself with God, seeking His assistance and guidance. This, with plenty of hard work, has made me what I am today, for I have never spent one cent in musical tuition, or ever had a teacher.

If we can get bandsmen to realise the sacredness of their calling we shall not have the careless playing, inattention and other evils that rob us of our power and usefulness. Can you imagine anyone giving his testimony or appealing to sinners in the half-hearted way that some bandsmen perform their duties?

The cause of Christ demands, and should have, the best. There was a time in our early experience when a few faithful comrades, with a drum and a few old brass instruments did able service for The Master, although their musical efforts were far from being proficient, but what they lacked musically was more than equalled spiritually by their deep sincerity.

While I have the deepest reverence for the glorious old bass drum and tambourine, yet I feel the time has come when these are insufficient to attract all classes of people to hear the Gospel. Every organisation that does not make progress soon begins to decline, and I feel that The Salvation Army has been a recognised organisation long enough to show at least some degree of musical efficiency; in fact, the public are within their right in expecting this from us after forty years of continued effort along these lines'.

This statement by George Darby was extracted from, '*Heralds of Victory*', with the kind permission of the author, Ronald W. Holz.

As will have been gleaned, George was always very passionate about his music. There were times when his bandsmen would see tears falling from his eyes when something they were playing touched him deeply. He composed many hymns for the band and the Male Chorus. Just occasionally George would allow his sense of fun to surface in his music, as with his 1914 Christmas Carol composition, '*Sleigh Ride*', which had an accompaniment of barking dogs and the thudding of hoofs, sound effects provided by enthusiastic members of the Band!

On the 30th March 1915, Elizabeth gave birth to a son, George Raymond, who, to avoid confusion with his father, would be known throughout his life as Ray.

Thomas Ramell died peacefully in his sleep on 2nd May 1915, at the age of 60. *5* His funeral was one of the largest ever seen in Folkestone due to the presence of Salvation Army personnel from all over Kent who lined the streets. *The Folkestone, Hythe, Sandgate and Cheriton Herald* of 8th May published a photograph of the funeral cortege passing down Dover Road beneath which appeared this report:

DEATH OF MR T. I. RAMELL
FOUNDER OF SALVATION ARMY BAND

We regret to record the death of Mr Thomas I. Ramell, of 135, Dover-road, who passed away after a long illness on Sunday last. He died peacefully in his sleep.

Mr Ramell, who was 60 years of age, was a native of London, but came to Folkestone at the age of ten with his uncle, under whom he worked in the coachbuilding business in Dover-road. During his life in Folkestone he became greatly interested in Salvation Army work, and was a great helper of the Folkestone Corps, being always ready to assist and promote the organisation to the best of his ability. He was the founder of the Folkestone Salvation Army Band and was its Bandmaster for 21 years. During that time he was also solo cornet, and retained that position after he retired from his post as Bandmaster eleven years ago. He was beloved by Salvationists, and he also had innumerable friends in the town.

The Funeral took place on Thursday afternoon and was a most impressive ceremony, full Salvation Army honours being given.

A funeral service, conducted by the adjutant, was held in the Salvation Army Temple, previous to the remains being removed from the deceased's residence. Large numbers of spectators and sympathisers lined the route to the cemetery and watched the procession as it slowly passed, the band playing, "The Dead March" in "Saul".

The coffin, which was of polished elm with brass fittings, was covered with wreaths and surmounted with the late bandsman's cap and cornet. It bore the inscription "Thomas Ingram Ramell. Died May 2nd, 1915. Aged 60 years".

Another service was conducted by the Adjutant (Mr Robert Edwards) at the graveside, and Bandmaster Pope, Bandmaster Grieg of Canterbury, and Mr C. Setterfield, Folkestone Treasurer, spoke briefly. Appropriate hymns were sung.

The chief mourners were:- Mrs T. I. Ramell (widow), Mr George Ramell (brother), Mr and Mrs Dalton, Mr and Mrs Dingle, Mr and Mrs Andrews (sons-in-law and daughters), Miss F. Ramell (daughter), and Sergt.-Instr. E. Turner (2nd Reserve, The Buffs). Several Employees from the works were also present. There were many beautiful floral tributes.

In July 1916, Elizabeth and George were promoted from Captain to Ensign, and George took over responsibilities with the Employment Agency at Territorial Headquarters.

With her marriage to George and the birth of a healthy child, Elizabeth had at last found the security and happiness which had eluded her for so many years. It was time to cement their new lives together and to ratify their status by becoming American citizens. George began the process on the 13th May 1916 when he completed a Declaration of Intention which, in part, read, 'It is my bona fide intention to renounce forever all allegiance and fidelity to any foreign prince, potentate, state or sovereignty, and particularly to George V King of Great Britain and Ireland of whom I am now a subject. I am not an anarchist; I am not a polygamist nor a believer in the practice of polygamy; and it is my intention in good faith to become a citizen of the United States of America and to permanently reside therein; so Help me God'. The Declaration was recorded with the reference number 12716.

Gravestone of Thomas Ingram, and later his wife Elizabeth Ramell.
(Author's Collection.)

The Darby Family circa 1917.
(Ruth E. Freeman and Ethel & Charles Edge Collections.)

The First World War continued to rage and in Washington DC on 6th April 1917 Congress passed the Declaration of War which, when signed that day by President Woodrow Wilson, formally signalled America's entry to the fighting. Within a short space of time the National Staff Band found its number severely depleted by those of its members who had volunteered for service in support of the troops at the front line. It wasn't until the end of the war in November 1918 that the Band was back up to full strength.

That was also the year that Pronouncement of Elizabeth and George's American Citizenship was made at the Supreme Court of the First Judicial District, Bronx, New York under certificate no. 914502. It was a step that was to be copied by Evangeline Booth some years later when she too changed nationality.

Also in 1918 the couple were promoted to Adjutant and negotiated the purchase of 2706 Heath Avenue in the Bronx. The house, just a five minute walk from the Marble Hill Subway Station, was to remain their home for the next thirty-five years.

2706 Heath Ave, The Bronx, New York, photographed in Nov 2001, by Debbie Danson, with the kind permission of Mr Ezequiel Hernandez. The original brickwork is now covered with a weatherproof siding.

'A WHALE OF A GOOD LAUGH'

Having settled into 2706 Heath Avenue it became apparent that Elizabeth and George enjoyed keeping their home life every bit as busy as the Ramell family home in Folkestone had been. For many years the couple took in lodgers who occupied rooms on the third floor. They were all bachelor members of the Salvation Army, and generally members of George's band.

Those who were sharing the house with them at the time of the 1920 US Census were Lt Leslie Arkett and his brother Edgar, Cameron Douglas, Walter Nice and Captain Catherine Miller. Elizabeth enjoyed cooking their meals and they in return loved her motherly ways. She described looking after the lodgers as, "Not just Christian Fellowship, but also a whale of a good laugh."

Shortly afterwards a lodger arrived who was to become a particular friend of the Darbys. William Slater had also been raised in a Staffordshire Salvationist family, in Cradely Heath twenty miles south of Cannock. When he was 14 his family had immigrated to Schenectady, New York State. William's father was an accomplished musician and had played with the renowned Black Dyke Mills Band. William also specialised on the euphonium and in his early twenties he underwent Officer Training and was farewelled to New York City to join the National Staff Band. He was to remain living with the Darbys until his own marriage.

In 1920, Elizabeth made a private visit to the two families in England taking five year old Raymond with her so he could meet his surviving grandparents for the first time. On completion of this vacation, they left Southampton on the 31st July aboard *S.S. Imperator*, seemingly unperturbed or possibly unaware that its master shared the same surname as the captain of the *Titanic*, Capt C. A. Smith!

The highlight the following year for the National Staff Band was an approach made to George Darby by the Aeolian Company of New York City who requested that the Band make some gramophone recordings for their Vocalion Record label. The first 12" 78rpm record was released in December that year and sold over 4,000 copies in its first week. An advertisement for the record in The War Cry is printed opposite.

Interesting that the record should contain the Band's arrangement of 'Nearer, My God, to Thee' - thought by many to be the last tune played by Wallace Hartley and his gallant band of musicians aboard the sinking

Titanic. It is most unlikely though that Elizabeth would have played any part in its selection for this recording. Due to the success of this first record a second was released the following March.

A further innovation occurred in 1923 during a Salvation Army Congress in Philadelphia, when the Band were asked to take part in their first live radio broadcasts. Both were sponsored by department stores, the first taking place in the organ loft at Wannamaker's and the second at the

Label of the 2nd recording, 'Memories/Excerpts from Haydn'. Pressed on brown shellac at the Aeolian Factory in Garwood NJ.

(Record held by the Salvation Army National HQ Archives and Research Center USA.)

studios of WFI-Radio, sponsored by Strawbridge Clothiers. Thereafter requests for recordings and radio appearances became commonplace. For young Raymond it must have been a delight to locally announce, "My Daddy's on the radio!"

Also in 1923, Elizabeth and George welcomed into their home George's younger sister, Mary, who had just emigrated under their sponsorship to the United States on *S.S. Aquitania*. Mary was found employment in the Welfare Department of the Salvation Army Headquarters and remained living with Elizabeth and George for three years until she also entered the Officers Training College. A second of George's sisters, Grace, would later join them before moving on to Ohio.

Mary Darby
(Ruth E. Freeman Collection.)

A memorable concert for George and the band took place on the weekend of 18-19th October 1924 during a visit to Washington D.C. They played before President and Mrs Calvin Coolidge at the White House.

The Darbys moved up again in rank, to Major, in 1925. The couple had for many years been enjoying visits at weekends and holidays to the seaside town of Belmar (formerly known as Ocean Beach. The name was changed in 1889 to Belmar- the French for Beautiful Sea), 60 miles south of New York along the New Jersey Monmouth County shoreline. There they would stay at the Kensington Home of Rest, a Salvation Army vacation home situated at 207 13th Avenue, between A & B Streets.

A postally used postcard of Ocean Ave and Boardwalk, Belmar NJ, 1934.

(Author's Collection.)

A picnic under the Belmar boardwalk, circa 1920.
Elizabeth with bathing cap, George against the right post and Ray infront of him.
(Ruth E. Freeman Collection.)

Whilst young, Ray Darby developed such a liking for scientific matters that his parents gave him a science set which included a microscope. Elizabeth was in the habit of eating the same lunch practically every day of her life - an apple, with bread and a particular variety of cheese.

One day Ray subjected a sample of the cheese to examination under the microscope and when he showed his mother the 'creepy crawly' results she vowed never to eat that variety again! Ray progressed with his interest and later in life was to serve a distinguished career as a Science Master.

Elizabeth and her young scientist.
(Ruth Freeman Collection.)

Both Elizabeth and George loved animals and one day visited the Bide-A-Wee Animal Shelter in New York. They brought home an Airedale Terrier puppy whom Ray named, 'Pal'. The dog was to become his constant companion, even to the extent of accompanying him during long swims off the beach at Belmar. Pal would be there furiously paddling alongside him. Whenever Pal wanted a biscuit he would sit and bark rather loudly. Elizabeth would say to him, "Too loud! Whisper" and Pal would then purse his lips and whimper to gain his reward.

Elizabeth with friend Violet Nice and 'Pal' on the Belmar boardwalk.
(Ruth E. Freeman Collection.)

Elizabeth and George Darby were, not unnaturally, deeply religious, but not to the extent of being fanatical. Their faith was a great source of strength to them and they each laid aside separate periods daily for prayers and devotion. Prior to every band concert he ever took part in George would briefly closet himself in prayer. It may not be fully understood by all that the Salvation Army is a Church first of all for its members, and the Social Services for which it is perhaps best known, are of secondary importance. Hence the Army saying, 'Heart to God and Hand to Man.'

George's allegiance to this doctrine once gave Elizabeth fears that his career was about to come to an abrupt end. In April 1926, General Bramwell Booth was in New York and addressed a meeting of the Officers' Council, attendance at which was mandatory for all serving Officers. As the General was speaking George gained the impression that he was emphasising the importance of the 'Hand to Man', more than the 'Heart to God'. Without hesitation or apology George stood up and loudly said, "The Salvation Army is first a Church". Elizabeth, who would never have dreamt of doing such a thing, went red as a beetroot and was pulling at the back of George's jacket and telling him, "George, sit down, for Heaven's sake!" It seemed that her whisper was heard all round the meeting. Realising the attention that had been drawn upon them both, Elizabeth, and Mary beside her, went an even brighter red. All was saved however when the General acknowledged his mistake and apologised for creating the wrong impression.

George's intervention that evening may not however have been quite as risqué as it might have first appeared. As a Major at the Territorial Headquarters at the time and a confidant of Commander Evangeline Booth he would have been privy to the growing unease amongst Senior Officers at a number of General Booth's policies, and his stated intention to personally decide his own successor, as William Booth had set out in his Deed of Constitution in 1878. Many thought that it was time that a more democratic course should be adopted. The matter was to be resolved two years later.

The end of May 1926, proved to be another traumatic period for Elizabeth and George with the receipt of a wire informing them of the death of George's mother, Lucy Darby at the age of 66 years. The couples' passports had expired and it was necessary for George to make application for renewal on 21st May. A joint passport was issued the following day and he sailed from New York on 26th, aboard *S.S. Aquitania* bound for Liverpool.

Elizabeth and George. Photographs and signatures from 1926.
(Phillip Gowan Collection.)

George's arrival back in Cannock on 2nd June was later reported in that week's edition of *The Cannock Advertiser* and the degree to which George was revered within his hometown Corps, even twenty years after he had moved to the USA, can be judged from *The Advertiser* article which read;

CANNOCK SALVATION ARMY

On Wednesday evening the young people's section of the Cannock Salvation Army Corps provided a free tea for 350 children in the Salvation Army Hall. The meal was naturally much appreciated by the youngsters.

In the evening the band played for a short period in the Market Square, but owing to the inclement weather the programme was considerably curtailed. The Band afterwards proceeded to the railway station to meet Major George Darby (late Bandmaster of the Cannock Band). He arrived by the 8.50 p.m. train and was accorded a rousing welcome. An adjournment was made to the Salvation Army Hall, where a short reception was held. Major Darby will attend the memorial service of his late mother to be held at the Salvation Army Hall on Sunday evening next.

On the 11th January 1928, Elizabeth and George attended Mary's wedding to Ensign Floyd Freeman who worked at that time alongside George at the Headquarters and was a member of the Staff Band and Male Chorus. The wedding took place in Brooklyn and the music for the service was played by the Band, the name of which had by then been changed to

Floyd Freeman and Mary Darby's Wedding. George second from left, Elizabeth second from right.
(Ruth E.Freeman Collection.)

the New York Staff Band (NYSB). They had to perform with a stand-in conductor on this occasion as George was busy giving his sister away. Elizabeth was also a member of the bridal party.

The Freemans' subsequent career saw them with appointments in New York, Boston and Altoona PA. On each occasion they worked in New York they would live either near or with the Darbys. On the 25th November 1929, the year in which Elizabeth and George were promoted to Brigadier, Mary gave birth to a daughter, Ruth Elizabeth. She had been named after Elizabeth and she grew up in the Darby household and came to dearly love her 'Aunt Bess' as she affectionately referred to Elizabeth. Ruth grew up to also adore her cousin Ray, 14 years her senior and can well recall the great sense of fun that the Darby family possessed. She obviously inherited the same sense of humour herself. An elderly artist with a long flowing white beard who was a regular visitor to the house and also attended Salvation Army meetings was referred to by the youngsters as 'Father Christmas'.

Ruth E. Freeman aged four years.
(Ruth E. Freeman Collection.)

In 1929, a Salvation Army High Council was convened in London to discuss General Bramwell Booth's deposition on the grounds of his ill health. The General had been unable to work at the International Headquarters for eight months. In his place, as the third General of the Army, the Council elected Commissioner Edward J. Higgins. One of his first moves was to change Evangeline Booth's rank from Commander to Commander-in-Chief.

The same year proved to be a challenging year for George as the Army had outgrown the old Headquarters building at 120-130 W. 14th Street and it was torn down to make way for a new building of improved design which incorporated an auditorium to seat 2,000, a young woman's' residence hotel to house 350, a gymnasium and a swimming pool. A temporary Headquarters was set up in a new office building at Broadway and 14th Street. On the 15th October the new cornerstone was laid by the Commander-in-Chief and the new building was completed within twelve months.

Within days of the laying of the cornerstone life in America for many was to change dramatically when the Stock Market crashed and the depression took a hold on the nation. Overnight the richest nation in the world suddenly found itself living on the breadline. The Salvation Army was put into a position where the increase in demand for its social services was counter-balanced by a diminishing income from endowments and company donations.

"No man need steal, starve, or commit suicide; come to the Salvation Army", was the Army's cry but the sheer numbers of those seeking help from the organisation over the next few years led to a situation by June 1932, when emergency relief funds were exhausted. Drastic measures had to be taken. A number of training establishments throughout America were closed for a year, and the already low salaries of Officers were cut by 10%. There were to be a few more years of austerity before the nation's economy took off once more.

When Elizabeth and Mary had first gone out shopping together they had sought to find the shortest routes to the shops they required to visit. They determined that the shortest routes meant cutting off as many corners as possible and thereafter, an invitation from Elizabeth to go shopping with her became, "Mary, let's go cut corners."

Elizabeth was a first-class cook and was well known for her culinary skills in the green-tiled kitchen at the rear of the second floor. She made all her own bread with wheat and white flour. It is little surprise that a regular meal she prepared was roast beef and Yorkshire pudding and she also excelled in the preparation of a number of chicken dishes. She did not believe in cooking any of her food by frying. Suet pudding was a favourite in the house having been wrapped in cheesecloth and steamed. After each meal in the oak panelled and ceiling beamed dining room, George would rise from the table, kiss Elizabeth on the cheek and say, "Nice dinner Darling." On occasions when the couple required to dine alone, the lodgers' meals would be sent upstairs from the kitchen on the dumbwaiter which accessed all three floors and the cellar. Each holiday the Darbys would invite elderly people around to share their table.

Elizabeth and George at home.
(Jerilyn Sunlin Collection.)

The treats that Elizabeth prepared in her kitchen are still recalled today by the daughter of her friend, Violet Nice. Dawn, now Mrs Robert Wolfenbarger, is emphatic that Elizabeth made the best lemon tarts she has ever tasted in her life.

Elizabeth and George were also, by nature, a very generous couple. It became a regular habit of theirs each December to send a Christmas cake that Elizabeth had made herself to each of their brothers and sisters back in England. One year George sent his brother Harry two gold watches, one for work and one for 'best'!

George was a first class handyman and rarely, if ever, had to resort to calling out a repairman. In the cellar he set up a workshop that contained every kind of tool necessary for any conceivable household emergency. With his electric band saw he made some of the furniture in the house and, as a hobby, he specialised in making wooden plates on which a friend would paint still life pictures.

Those that George kept were displayed on a plate rack high on the sitting room wall at the front of the apartment. It was in this room that Elizabeth kept her sewing machine and George had his piano and an array of brass instruments.

'THERE'S NOT THE SLIGHTEST NEED TO SING!'

Quite often the residents of 2706 Heath Avenue would take an outing to the local swimming baths. Elizabeth never accompanied them, preferring to remain at home. During bad winters when the streets of New York were covered in snow they could all be found tobogganing together down the slopes of Kingsbridge Road at the rear of Heath Avenue. Some years later when Ruth was of an age to enjoy the same fun with her friends on their 'Flexible Flyers', it was a much more perilous pursuit due to the presence of "motor trolleys and automotive vehicles", that had increased in number in the area.

Ruth and Ray loved to wrestle together and Ray was under instructions from his mother to ensure that whenever this happened he was to wear his oldest shirt as these rough house sessions usually resulted in tears to his clothes.

With an occasional change of lodgers it was necessary to maintain some kind of order in the premises and house rules were dispensed with humour as a sign which hung above the bathtub in the bathroom for many years testified, it read;

> *Please remember, don't forget,*
> *Never leave the bathroom wet.*
> *Nor leave the soap still in the water,*
> *That's a thing you never ought'a.*
> *And, as if you'd do the thing,*
> *There's not the slightest need to sing!*

The lodgers devised their own method of returning the humour. While the Band were out at concerts, and often at Elizabeth's instigation, as George was on the podium about to raise his baton one of the members would give a prepared signal and the Band would start to play. George would thus be forced to hurriedly catch up with them. Afterwards he would always laugh about it as heartily as the perpetrators.

When not engaged in her Womens' Services Elizabeth spent a good deal of time at her sewing machine on which she made all her own clothes, including overcoats and her uniforms. Every Saturday afternoon she could be found busy at her sewing listening to the Metropolitan Opera House wireless broadcasts. Her favourite opera was Verdi's '*Aida*' and she also particularly enjoyed *Beethoven's 9th Symphony*. There wasn't anything that delighted Elizabeth more as a gift than material to make a new dress. She adored her sewing and finally had so many dresses that George put up an iron bar in the bedroom that stretched from one side of the room to the other. Elizabeth made a curtain to cover up the dresses which George then referred to as the 'iron curtain'.

During the 1930s it became commonplace for women to wear slacks but Elizabeth, and Mary, retained their Victorian standards and were never seen in anything other than skirts and dresses. Neither did they ever wear bright colours although they did consider this to be acceptable for the young. Ruth and her friends however preferred to wear 'earth tone' colours. Whenever Elizabeth saw them wearing grey she would tease them that they were dressed in "prison grey!" George was also one for standing by his traditions. No one around him dare even make the suggestion that female musicians should be allowed to join the New York Staff Band.

The Darby family continued to make regular weekend and vacation visits to Belmar and such became their affinity with the town that in the mid 1930s they purchased real estate in 13th Avenue. Together with another Salvation Army couple, Col and Mrs William Palmer, they arranged for the construction of a property which was built to their own specifications. The result was a duplex (semi-detached) property which shared a common basement and became 315 A&B 13th Avenue. The plot of

The Belmar Avenues all had houses of similar design. This was 8th Ave in 1929.
(Author's Collection.)

land was so large that George was able to do as many others in the avenue had done and build a small bungalow at the rear. Each summer the population of Belmar quadrupled with the numbers of visitors who vacationed there. The bungalow meant that the house could be rented out during the summer months and the family still had somewhere for themselves to stay. The choice of a seaside town for their vacation home was surely a reflection of Elizabeth's love of coastal life and a reminder of her upbringing in Folkestone.

The Darbys' duplex still stands today and I am most grateful to the present occupier, Dana Smith and her family, for permission to reproduce this photograph.

315 A and B 13ᵗʰ Avenue Belmar. (Again, observe the weatherproof siding.)
(Dana Smith Collection.)

Whenever they stayed at the house in Belmar the Darbys would enjoy the short stroll to the beach every evening after their meal. When the Freemans were with them Elizabeth and Floyd would sit on benches by the beach whilst George and Mary more energetically walked the mile-long boardwalk. Elizabeth deemed the two pairs, "The Sitters and the Walkers!"

Amongst the many people in Belmar with whom the Darbys became friends were Mr and Mrs George Messina, and their young daughters Marie (Mimi) and Gertrude who lived opposite the couple at 314 13th Avenue. Today Mimi, now Mrs Biaggio Uricoli, clearly recalls the great thrill it was for her as a young girl to see cars with license plates from so many different US States parking up outside the Kensington Home of Rest. She would often see George and Elizabeth walking about in their Salvation Army uniforms. She remembers them as a wonderful family, lovely people and delightful to talk to.

George was keen on tennis and after each occasion he played he would leave his tennis balls, then in short supply, on their porch for them to use. Later in life it did not escape the girls' attention that Ray was a handsome lifeguard. They were pleased to also be his friend.

In June 1931, George relinquished his leadership of the New York Staff Band. An entry in the Secretary's Desk in *The War Cry* of 17th January that year listed Brigadier Darby amongst a number of officers who had suffered through ill health and were 'somewhat indisposed'. No other mentions of illness are recorded and George was to live until the age of 83. In his excellent book, *'Heralds of Victory'*, a history of the New York Staff Band, author Ronald Holz intimates that stories of ill health may have been a subterfuge to divert from the fact that Evangeline Booth had argued with Darby over his continued use of 'outside music', although he had greatly curtailed this as better Army music became more available and more abundant.

He, in return, may have quarrelled with her over legal matters pertaining to the High Council that deposed her brother, Bramwell. George Darby remained a member of the Headquarters family, carrying out major administrative responsibilities until his retirement but be was rarely brought back into the musical limelight and certainly not at Evangeline's behest.

On the 27th June 1931, Elizabeth boarded the *S.S. Minnekahda* at New York at the start of another visit to England. It is likely that she brought Ray with her for a visit that was to last for the entire summer vacation.

In 1933, George became the Property Secretary and also received the Long Service Order. The Property Department was a large one and embraced a variety of issues such as all Salvation Army Legal matters, an Architectural Section, Workmen's Compensation, Army Vehicle Insurance Office and a General Office. The 18th February 1933 edition of *The War Cry* carried an article beneath pictures of Elizabeth and George which read: *'Of interest to War Cry readers is the appointment by the General and the Commander-in-Chief, on the recommendation of Commissioner John McMillan, of Brigadier George Darby to be the Property Secretary for the Eastern Territory, succeeding Lt.-Colonel Vernon Post, whose appointment as Eastern Territorial Men's Social Service Secretary was recently announced. By reason of more than nine years as first assistant to the Property Secretary and his splendid training in departmental work in general, the Brigadier brings to the position keen executive ability, a wide range of knowledge, judgment and wisdom'.*

The article continued by giving a resume of George's career and concluded: '*In addition to creditably filling these responsible positions, the Brigadier was for nearly two decades the bandmaster of the Staff Band. During those years his brilliant leadership made the aggregation one of the outstanding musical groups in The Salvation Army world.*

Mrs Brigadier Darby has also been connected with the Army all of her life, being dedicated at Folkestone, England, where her father, in 1883, organized the corps band. Prior to her marriage in 1913 she had served for a brief time in the Women's Social Service Department. For the past few years she has been an active worker in the League of Mercy, a branch of service in which she takes keen interest and pleasure and one in which she proves herself the soul of devotion and faithfulness. She is also one of the survivors of the Titanic *disaster of 1912.*'

There was great excitement in New York in September 1934 when news came through from the Salvation Army High Council in London that Evangeline Booth had been elected to serve as the fourth General of the Army - the first woman to be elected to that office. President Franklin D. Roosevelt cabled congratulations on behalf of the entire nation. As accustomed as she was to grand receptions even Evangeline Booth could not have failed to be surprised at the reception that awaited her upon her return to New York aboard the *S.S. Leviathan*.

A flotilla of flagged craft crowded the harbour with banners reading, 'WELCOME HOME, GENERAL EVANGELINE BOOTH'.

Rose petals were dropped from overhead aircraft. Mayor Fiorello La Guardia headed a reception committee made up of 250 prominent New York citizens. Manhattan gave Evangeline its highest honour - a ticker-tape parade. At the City Hall the proceedings were broadcast live on the radio. Her departure the following month to start work from the London Headquarters met with similar scenes.

Clifford Greene could remember meeting his Aunt Elizabeth on a solo visit she made to Folkestone in 1935, the year in which the Darbys were promoted to Lieutenant Colonel. On this occasion she had travelled across on the *S.S. Berengaria* which had left New York on the 8th May.

He recalled that he liked her immediately and found her warm, friendly, outgoing and caring. It was obvious then to him as a 16 year old, that she had a zest for life and living, and he was also quick to find that she possessed a great sense of humour. They made some wonderful outings in her company during that visit and enjoyed walking by the sea and over the hills surrounding Folkestone.

Elizabeth with her mother and sisters, strolling Folkestone beach.
Left to right: Florence Green, Beatrice Dingle, Winifred Andrews,
Elizabeth Ramell and Elizabeth.
(The photograph was taken by Edith, the fifth sister.
(Clifford Greene Collection.)

Clifford's younger sister, now Mrs June Fuger, was 12 at the time of Elizabeth's visit and thought that her aunt was a rather formidable lady. She still recalls Elizabeth's annoyance upon hearing that her mother's brother George, who was then in his 70s, was 'living in sin' with his lady friend. Elizabeth went to see the couple and denounced their scandalous behaviour. A wedding was hastily arranged and took place prior to Elizabeth's return to America!

Elizabeth also took part in many Salvation Army activities during her stay. Clifford remembered that his Aunt's favourite flowers were primroses. She had, after each visit to her family, taken primrose plants back to America but found that they were unsuitable to grow in the soil at her own home.

The dumbwaiter at the house in Heath Avenue was invaluable for passing items between the Freemans on the first floor, the Darbys on the second and the lodgers above them. When the doors were open it also served as a handy voice tunnel for passing messages as sound travelled through it well. Ruth had obviously forgotten this one day when, as a youngster and a promising student of the Julliard School of Music, she started to play a jazz tune on the family piano. George, who did not

Elizabeth and her Mother. *8*
(Clifford Greene Collection.)

appreciate the music of the day, dashed into the room and mockingly placed his hands around her neck. He in turn was attacked by Ruth's dog who grabbed his ankle. The mock assault ended rather rapidly, but so did the playing of jazz at 2706!

Some years later, when Ruth wanted her first car, her parents were very reticent to give their permission. It was Aunt Bess who persuaded them that she should have her wish and she and Uncle George gave Ruth one third of the purchase price of the new Renault.

Ray Darby grew up to be a great credit to his parents. Ruth states that although he spoke very little of religion his life was certainly indicative of that of a decent Christian. He was a man who was dearly loved by all who knew him.

Ray's first work experience as a young lad was as a kitchen hand at the Kensington Home of Rest in Belmar. He had inherited his father's musical prowess and became proficient with a number of instruments. His major activity however was sport, particularly swimming. Later in life at New York University he studied science and was a member of the swimming team and also captained the water polo team. Elizabeth would often go to see him swim. One day she was sitting near the edge of the pool when Ray surfaced right in front of her after a gruelling swim. He appeared cross-eyed and disorientated and gasping for breath. Elizabeth never went again.

As a teenager, Ray joined the lifeguard service on the ocean beach at Belmar. He was based at the 16th Avenue station where he later attained the position of Captain of the Guard. He graduated from University with an Advanced Degree in Chemistry and immediately obtained a position as a Chemistry Master at the Fieldstone High School for Boys in Riverdale, Bronx.

After marrying, he made his family home across the Hudson River in East Clifton Avenue, Tenafly, New Jersey, just 12 miles from the Bronx. His parents-in-law also had a holiday home in Belmar so he was often in the town and continued with his lifeguard duties well into his forties. Visitors today to the Boathouse Bar and Grill, 1309 Main St. Belmar, can see around the walls a display of vintage photograph of the town's lifeguards - several show Ray Darby.

Ray Darby on Graduation Day. [6]
(Ruth E. Freeman Collection.)

When Ruth was in her teens she was diagnosed with a disabilitating condition. It was her Aunt Bess who spent a great deal of time with her, reassuring her and helping her to prepare for her future. Ruth has never forgotten these kindnesses. Ruth says that her own favourite Bible quotation, from the Book of Micah, Chapter 6, Verse 8, exemplifies the way that her Aunt and Uncle lived their lives. 'And what doth the Lord require of thee, but to do justly and to love mercy and to walk humbly with thy God.'

Ruth E. Freeman

Elizabeth Darby was admitted to the Long Service Order on the 9th June 1938 having served a long and distinguished career with the Home League, and the League of Mercy in the New York area where her work had brought her into contact with the weak, the poor and the suffering. On 19th July 1939 the many years of devoted service by Elizabeth and George was recognised with their promotion to Colonel.

On the 7th April 1941, the couple enjoyed a memorable day when their son Raymond married his sweetheart, Miss Kathleen Elizabeth James. It was George who officiated at the wedding which was held at the James' residence in Montclair, New Jersey.

Elizabeth Darby, William L. James, Col William Palmer, Best Man unknown, Raymond and Kathleen, George Darby, Marilyn James, Brig Edith Nice, Evelyn James.
(Jerilyn Sunlin Collection.)

'BROTHER DARBY WILL ADDRESS THE CONGREGATION'

In 1943 a group of Royal Navy personnel travelled from England on the *S.S. Mauritania* to Canada to undertake flying training for the newly formed Royal Navy Air Branch (later to become the Fleet Air Arm). Included in the party was 18 year old Leading Seaman Ronald Darby, the son of George's cousin Frank. Prior to departure the family had written ahead to George and this had resulted in an open invitation for Ron to visit New York. He was unable to get away from the training at Christmas but well recalls that the Salvation Army in St. Thomas kindly provided all of the servicemen with a welcome Christmas meal of bacon and eggs.

Granted some leave in the New Year he and a colleague, Leading Seaman Emmett, journeyed to New York and received a warm welcome from the Darbys at their Bronx home. Not only of course were the Darbys pleased to welcome family visitors but they were also keen to learn first hand of the latest news from war-torn Europe. Ron recalls that Elizabeth struck him as a quiet, reserved and motherly woman who was quite happy to remain in the background of things.

A/LA John Emmett, A/LA Ron Darby and Colonel George Darby snapped outside 2706 Heath Avenue.
(Ron Darby Collection.)

It was primarily George who escorted the two servicemen around the sights of the City, showing them the Empire State Building, the Statue of Liberty and other attractions, and also took them skating. Seeing as they were servicemen on leave George did take them on one special outing - to a burlesque show at the Roxy Theatre. No doubt an interesting evening, and certainly not an expensive one as the Roxy Theatre allowed free admission to Servicemen in uniform.

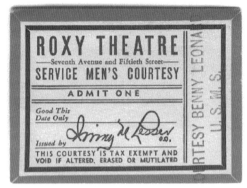

(Author's Collection.)

Ruth can still recall taking the men out with her on one occasion and the sight of her with a handsome uniformed sailor on each arm caused a great deal of envy amongst her friends!

Postcard of the 6,200 seater Roxy Theatre, NY.
(Author's Collection.)

Ron Darby still possesses the programme for a Salvation Army gathering which he attended with Elizabeth and George on the evening of Sunday, 2nd January 1944. The meeting, held at the Riverside Church, Riverside Drive and 122nd Street, is particularly edged in Ron's memory as, halfway through the proceedings the minister, a Dr Hellstrom, asked the congregation to greet Brother Darby from Cannock, England, and stated that if time permitted he would be addressing them at the conclusion of the evening. Ron, totally unaware and unprepared for such an eventuality sat nervously for the remainder of the service which fortunately overran and therefore relieved him of the task.

After so many years of research with frequent mentions of the mischievous humour of Elizabeth and George it makes me wonder if this was not yet a further example! Following their return to Canada, where winter conditions that year were extreme, Ron was delighted to find himself the recipient of regular parcels of food and warm clothing sent from Heath Avenue.

Following the successful completion of his flying training in Tiger Moth and Harvard aircraft, Ron was granted a further leave period between the 9th and 13th April 1944. He again took the train to New York with Emmett and, not wishing to impose any further on the Darbys, the pair sought to

A studio portrait of the group taken at the Salvation Army Headquaters.
(Ron Darby Collection.)

book into a Salvation Army Hostel. There they were recognised and a call was made to George (listed in the Bronx telephone directory under the entry, 'DARBY George Rev. Kingsbge 63675') who arrived shortly afterwards and insisted that they again stay at the house. Recalling

Three generations: George, Raymond and Little Ray, circa 1944.
(Jerilyn Sunlin Collection.)

Elizabeth's cooking skill Ron was happy to comply. Ron was aware of Elizabeth's involvement with the Titanic from his family back in England but he is certain that at no time during the few days he spent in her company did anyone raise the subject. *7*

During the war years Elizabeth, in addition to her other duties, took an active part in the 'Bundles for Britain' campaign - the parcelling up and despatch of food and other items that were in short supply in the British Isles. She also spent many hours knitting gloves and scarves for use by the Allied Forces.

The war years were also to become memorable to the Darby's for a welcome new role in life – when they became grandparents. Their first grandchild, Raymond Lewis (Little Ray) was born on the 2nd January 1942 and his sister Jerilyn on the 13th February 1944.

Elizabeth and George, August 1945.
(Dalton Family Collection.)

'I REMEMBER EVERY MOMENT OF THAT NIGHT'

By the time of the Darbys' retirement, public interest in the story of the *Titanic* had all but disappeared. A couple of events were about to take place though which were to return the name *Titanic* back to the world stage. The first of these was a decision made in 1952, by 20th Century Fox Film Corporation to make a movie based on the disaster. As part of their preparations, they contacted a number of survivors, including Elizabeth, and asked for their memories of the night of 14th/15th April 1912.

Elizabeth replied to their request with the following handwritten statement:

The Greatest peacetime shipwreck 1912

I remember every moment of that night, very well, my name was then Elizabeth Nye, was travelling alone, returning to New York from a visit to my home and family in Folkestone, England. On account of a coal strike then in England I was transferred from another ship to the Titanic, which would have to sail on her maiden voyage to New York on April 10th. I was placed very comfortably in a second class cabin with three other young women, "one of whom I am still in touch with."

On Sunday the 14th it became very cold, we could not stay out on deck, so we all came together in the dining room, for a hymn sing, finished up by singing, "O hear us when we cry to Thee, for those in peril on the sea," little dreaming of our own peril soon to be. We four were settled for the night by 11pm and about 40 minutes later I heard a loud scraping noise, the great ship shivered and stopped. We had been going 28 knots an hour, the sudden silence seemed strange and yet the impact was so slight the three girls slept through it. Men were running by our door. I got up, put on a skirt & coat & slippers, went to the deck, in time to see the iceberg glide slowly by, a great white mountain.

The stewards shouted 'There is nothing to worry about, this ship could not possibly sink, she is a lifeboat in herself, but we must go to the boats & get off, to lighten the ship so that the water tight doors could be closed.

The ship began to tilt & people looked worried and afraid. Then came the order "Man the lifeboats - Woman and children first" Neither the boatmen or the passengers had had a boatdrill, & yet there was no panic, we took our time. I was told to go to my cabin & put on my lifebelt, there was one for every person aboard, but only 20 lifeboats each built for 65 persons. I met my roommates on the stairs, they had been called up then the door locked behind them, it was no use to go down so I lost all my belongings. I found my stewardess, she fastened a belt on me & I put one on her, we went to the deck together, she never got off.

I went to the side where the last boat was being lowered. I stood there looking at a crowd of men huddled together, a silent crowd, while the ship's orchestra of ten young men were standing knee deep in water playing a tune called 'Autumn.' The words are:

> God of mercy and compassion,
> Look with pity on my pain,
> Hold me up in mighty waters,
> Keep my eyes on things above,
> Peace and everlasting love,
> Nearer my God to Thee.

Someone called out, "Here is another woman!" and I was pushed into the boat. Blankets were thrown in after *me, for we had four babies without their mothers, they were reunited on the rescue ship.*

We watched the portholes slowly disappearing and the S.O.S. rockets shooting upwards, until one end of the ship dipped into the sea. Nobody could stand on deck, hundreds jumped or fell. Then we heard the terrible cry for the boats to come back and pick them up.

Their lifebelts kept them up until death came by freezing, more than 1,500 perished. Plenty of time but no boats, only 20 for 2,200 people and some were overturned with women and children, no men to pull the oars.

The sky was alight with stars, but the sea looked like black ink. I don't remember being afraid, but I thought what a horrible way to die, in that black icy water. We saw the lights of the Carpathia at about 4 a.m. and it took us two hours to get to her, we had drifted so far away, she was waiting for us at the spot where the Titanic went down.

Letter reproduced with the kind permission of Walter Lord.

Filming of 20th Century Fox's movie, *Titanic*, which starred Barbara Stanwyck, Clifton Webb, Thelma Ritter, Robert Wagner and Audrey Dalton, began at their studios in November 1952 and was completed within the 50 days allotted. Post production had been carried out in time for the movie to receive it's World Premiere in April the following year during the anniversary week of the actual disaster. The event was held under the banner of 'Operation *Titanic*' and was hosted by the Naval Station Norfolk, Virginia.

The film company issued invitations to thirty-five movie critics, show business reporters and photographers from New York to cover the premiere and hired a National Airlines Flagship to take them from Idlewild Airport (today known as John F. Kennedy International) to Norfolk. The sight of so many members of the media making a mass exodus from the city was itself deemed newsworthy and their departure was filmed and shown on the evening news on WPIX and NBC Channel 4. Passengers on the flight included Ed Sullivan (the newspaper columnist who for 6 years had been hosting the Sunday night TV show, '*Toast of the Town*' and which in 1955 was renamed, '*The Ed Sullivan Show*'), and the veteran actor Charles Coburn.

A second flight arrived at the Naval Base carrying Fox executives from California. They brought with them, not the stars of Titanic, but a clutch of other Hollywood celebrities including Debra Paget, Anne Francis, Byron Palmer, Jeffrey Hunter and Nanette Fabray. The actors undertook a busy schedule on the 11th with a morning visit to the patients in the Base Hospital. The afternoon found them taking part in a mock amphibious landing on the '*Titanic* Beach' from LCVPs (Landing Craft, Vehicles, Personnel) supported by an aerial umbrella formed by squadrons of jet fighters.

The second phase of 'Operation *Titanic*' - the world premiere of *Titanic* - was staged with equal colour and excitement when several thousand personnel from the Base jammed into the already overflowing Shelton Theatre. The celebrities were introduced from the stage prior to the screening. This was followed by dinner in The Officers' Club which in turn was followed by the Navy Relief Ball. A formal charity affair it attracted several hundred leading military and civilian citizens from Norfolk and beyond. Debra Paget and Anne Francis were crowned during the Ball by Ed Sullivan as 'Co-Queens of the Atlantic Fleet'.

Several scenes from the movie were subsequently shown on '*Toast of the Town*' on May 3rd and a Movietone News report of 'Operation *Titanic*', entitled, '*Titanic Premiere Thrills South*' was shown at cinemas nationwide prior to the movie opening at 300 cinemas coast-to-coast on 13th May 1953.

Today, 50 years on, Anne Francis relates that the Studio contractees were required to go to so many movie premieres that her memories of them are mostly one big blur of limos, interviewers, blaring speakers and red carpets. Of the Titanic premiere however she can recall that it was the only one she ever attended that required her to take part in a simulated amphibious landing!

Prior to the official public opening of *Titanic* a special showing was held in New York to which a number of survivors of the actual disaster were invited. Elizabeth was one of the VIP guests and she was, as she said in a letter back to her sister Edith, "Delighted to have met up again at the premiere with one of the women with whom I shared a berth on the Titanic. We had known each other right away despite the passing of 41 years. Three other survivors who had also been rescued from the same lifeboat were there that night."

The cabin companion whom Elizabeth referred to was Mrs Selena Rogers, who was then living in Waverley, Pennsylvania, and at her request the other survivors, including Edith Russell, Frank Aks and his mother Leah, and Thomas McCormack who had been on the *Titanic* as a third class passenger travelling to New York, all signed her film brochure. Elizabeth added her New York contact address and the two women corresponded together for the remainder of their lives. An article about this special screening appeared in the May 18th edition of Life magazine under the heading 'SURVIVORS WATCH THE TITANIC GO DOWN AGAIN' The article featured on Leah Aks and her son Frank and mentioned that a total of 11 survivors had attended the screening but it did not name them all.

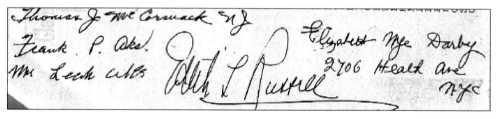

The signatures entered in Mrs Rogers programme.
(Ed Kamuda/Titanic Historical Society Collection.)

Titanic was a hybrid film, that is, that it placed the story of a fictional family aboard the factual event. The film was a box office success and earned its producer, Charles Brackett, and script writers, Walter Reisch and Richard Breen, the Oscar for Best Original Screenplay the following year.

When the film was later shown at the Folkestone Odeon cinema the local paper, by then renamed *The Folkestone Herald*, published an article with a photograph of Elizabeth headed 'Titanic Sea Disaster of 41 Years Ago - Folkestone Woman Was Among The Rescued'. They reminded their readers of Elizabeth's presence on the doomed ship and gave a resume of her life and career. They also took opportunity again to reprint Elizabeth's '*Carpathia* letter.'

The second event was to have an even greater and longer lasting effect on public awareness of the *Titanic* than the 20th Century Fox movie. A young copy writer and editor in a New York Advertising Agency, Walter Lord, was persuaded by friends to write a book about the *Titanic* disaster. As a young lad, Walter's parents had taken him to Europe aboard the *S.S. Olympic* and he had been fascinated ever since then by the tale of her ill-fated sister ship. By the mid-fifties he had authored a number of books about maritime matters and American history, and, interestingly, the lyrics

Folkestone & Hythe Herald
Advertisement.
(Author's Collection.)

to '*The Third Man Theme.*' Walter, using a research method he had used on his earlier projects, wrote letters to the editors of newspapers throughout the major cities in the United States and the United Kingdom appealing for survivors of the disaster to contact him to relate their memories of that night.

Walter's appeal in the New York press did not come to Elizabeth's notice but a friend of hers in the UK, Miss Margery W. Wilson of Birmingham, saw his letter and wrote to Mr Lord to advise him of Elizabeth's presence in his area.

Contact was made and in her reply of 14th June 1955, Elizabeth enclosed a copy of the same statement that she had earlier written for 20th Century Fox. A short period of correspondence followed after which it appears that Elizabeth, who by this time was in failing health, decided to lay her *Titanic* involvement to rest. In mid October she did receive a surprise invitation to attend a survivors' luncheon in New York. The invitation was sent by Washington Dodge Jr who, as a four year old child had been travelling in First Class with his parents on the *Titanic*. All three had been saved. Elizabeth was in two minds as whether to attend or not and did not initially reply to the invitation.

Her interest, however, was revived some days later with the publication of the November issue of the influential womens magazine, '*Ladies' Home Journal*'. The edition featured a lengthy 40 page extract from Walter Lord's book about the disaster, '*A Night to Remember*'.

Elizabeth found that the extract included the chapter in which she herself is mentioned. She much enjoyed the style of Mr Lord's book describing it as, "a most remarkable writing." As the author himself told the magazine, "I tried to re-create, minute by minute, the night the *Titanic* went down because I think it is the most exciting dramatic news story that ever happened. I didn't try to analyze anything technical. You just live with these people as they go through the supreme test of their lives." The book condensation prompted Elizabeth to write to Washington Dodge Jr accepting his invitation.

In mid November, Elizabeth, in common with the other 62 survivors who had assisted Walter Lord, received a signed copy of, 'A *Night to Remember*'. In a letter dated 15th November she wrote, "Dear Mr Lord. Thank you very much for your autographed copy of your book, 'A *Night to Remember*'. It will be kept in the Darby family. My son and his two children and their children, I'm sure, will appreciate it as the years go by. The book is well written. I remember every moment of that night even after 43 years have passed. Thank you for your kind thought. I remain yours sincerely, Elizabeth Darby".

Letter: Titanic Historical Society Archives
(Reprinted with the kind permission of Ed Kamuda.)

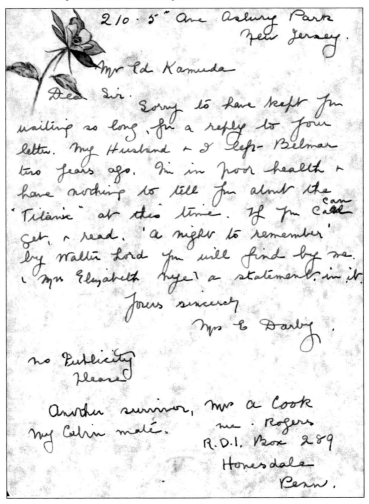

The survivors' luncheon took place on 21st November 1955 at the Commodore Hotel, New York City. Elizabeth attended accompanied by her Salvation Army colleague Violet Nice. Walter Lord had been sent an invitation but it is thought he had been unable to attend as, when this author met with him in his E 68th Street apartment in New York in March 1997, he confirmed that he had never had the pleasure of meeting with Elizabeth Darby. The luncheon was to be Elizabeth's last public acknowledgement of her past.

It seems that the label, '*Titanic* Survivor', had always rested very uneasily with Elizabeth. She spoke very rarely of the *Titanic* and '*The Musician*', a Salvation Army publication, was to later say that the rest of her life was a constant fight against the consequences of the shock and exposure which she endured in the tragedy. After the help that she volunteered to 20th Century Fox and Walter Lord, it is known that she turned down many other requests to make contributions to books and to be interviewed for radio and television programmes. In reply to a letter from Ed Kamuda of the *Titanic* Enthusiasts of America (later renamed the *Titanic* Historical Society) Elizabeth sent the reply, *(see page 119)*, in which she politely declined to add anything to the previous statement that she had made due to poor health. She marked her letter, 'No Publicity Please'.

No doubt Elizabeth felt that at the age of 70 she had given all she could give on the subject and wished it to become a closed chapter of her life. Her decision was fully supported by her husband.

Clifford Greene recalled that when he had met his Aunt she would always briefly answer any question put to her about the tragedy but she herself would never be the first to raise the subject.

Elizabeth was shy by nature and she could never have addressed large groups from a public platform not even at Salvation Army meetings. She was however at ease addressing small groups such as the Women's Home League, meetings where she was in control. It is known that in the 1920/30s she did speak at such meetings about her Titanic experiences and on each occasion she would take with her some of the items of clothing that she had been wearing the night the *Titanic* sank.

Elizabeth and George. August 1953.
(Ethel and Charles Edge Collection.)

'HAVING QUITE A TIME TO FIT THINGS IN'

In 1946, Senior Captain Lois Hargreaves was appointed to the Property Department as Office Manager. Today, over 60 years on, and now a retired Colonel, Lois still speaks of Elizabeth and George Darby with great fondness. She describes George as a fine Christian gentleman and she can still recall his greeting to her when she joined the Department. "Lois, I'm glad you're here," he said, "Please put the filing system in order and bring the office up-to-date. I'll back you all the way."

With trust like that Lois made sure she worked hard to justify the confidence he had placed in her. During the year she spent working with Colonel Darby she never once saw him angry or upset.

Elizabeth would occasionally visit the office. As the Colonel's wife she was entitled to take her midday meal with George in the Senior Officers Dining Room but, in her quiet and unassuming way, she always preferred to eat a simple packed lunch in the office with one of her friends. In the afternoon the two women would make the journey to Long Island to visit a former colleague who had been committed to a mental home.

George himself was increasingly busy writing the Minutes for The Board of Trustees and working on complex corporate legal matters. The Salvation Army had originally classed the six New England States as a Province but

The Colonels Darby shortly before retirement.
(Salvation Army National HQ Archives and Research Center USA.)

they were now to become Independent Divisions. It was George who prepared the necessary legal documentation for each State to have its own Corporation. He was the main liaison between the Salvation Army and their legal advisers, an eminent firm of New York lawyers. Indeed, such was the amount of legal knowledge acquired and exhibited by George that when his retirement was imminent the law firm offered him a position. He did not take the offer seriously and moved on to his last Army appointment, that of Secretary to the National Commander, Commissioner Edward J. Parker.

In September 1948, Elizabeth and George Darby retired from active service with the Salvation Army with the rank of full Colonel.

The Darbys appear to have elected initially for a 'semi-retirement' lifestyle as they remained living in New York for a further five years. Elizabeth carried on with her hospital visits and George busied himself with other Salvation Army matters. George had qualified as a driver in his 20s but Elizabeth had never learned to drive. All the vehicles that George had driven during his service had belonged to the Salvation Army so it was not until their retirement that the couple purchased their first motor car. They did so in joint ownership with Mary and Floyd.

To keep his mind active George, each Wednesday evening, would attend the Ford Forum where issues of the day were discussed before the public by a panel of experts.

The Darbys did install a television set in their home when it became fashionable to do so. George enjoyed watching classical music concerts whenever they were screened but Elizabeth preferred to remain faithful to her radio broadcasts which did not visually distract from her sewing and letter writing.

Elizabeth and George outside the cottage in their garden at 315.
(Ruth E. Freeman Collection.)

Since her first arrival in the Americas she had always been a prolific letter writer and had kept in regular contact with their many relatives and friends back in England. We can be sure however that the couple were both watching the television one evening in October 1951 when a 10 piece ensemble from the New York Staff Band made their first television appearance. This was followed in March 1952 with the full band appearing in their own half-hour presentation on WNBC-TV. From then on TV appearances became a regular occurrence.

The early years of the 1950s saw both Elizabeth and George reach the age of 70. It was time to sell their house in New York and relocate to their Belmar home. The couple had been natural hoarders all their married lives and rarely threw anything away that had come into their possession. As they prepared for the move south, Ray was to joke that in order to move everything they would need to hire a Mack Trailer Truck (articulated lorry). A view seemingly endorsed by Elizabeth when, on April 25th 1953, she posted a postcard of the new Salvation Army Officers' Retirement Home in Asbury Park to George's brother Harry, in Cannock. On it she wrote:

'Dear Family, We have sold our New York house and moved to Belmar. Having quite a time to fit things into smaller rooms but will get there. We are all well & hope everything is OK with you. Our SA Home is lovely, we may finish up there.

Lovingly, Bess and George.'

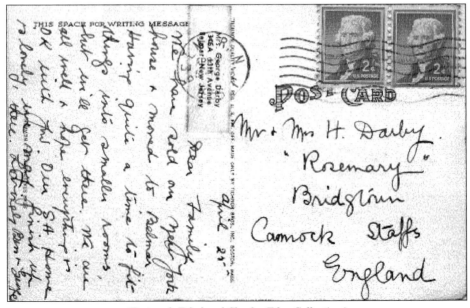

(Postcard: Ethel and Charles Edge Collection.)

'AND NOW I SAY, "PLEASE LORD, TAKE ME HOME"'

Eventually the move was completed and the couple settled into the quiet environment of Belmar. Unable, and indeed unwilling, to break their lifetime commitment of service to others they became voluntary helpers at a local Veterans Home. In addition, Elizabeth would run errands for some elderly neighbours who were unable to leave their house. They also became active members of their nearest Salvation Army Corps at Asbury Park.

In her sitting room, Elizabeth had a display cabinet in which she kept a number of items of Folkestone memorabilia. She had collected these during her trips back to the town of her birth. Pride of place was given to an antique figurine of a young Dutch boy sitting in a highchair. It was a tobacco jar which had belonged to her grandfather Frederick Ramell.

Elizabeth and George continued to make regular visits to the Kensington Home of Rest right up to its closure in 1956. There they would enjoy meeting up with the many old friends they had made during their service years. Special friends, invariably those who also shared English backgrounds, would be invited back to 315A for the treat of tea with home made bread. Although the couple had lived in America for over 50 years they had lost little of their English accents and had also retained many English mannerisms such as the love of gardening, the consideration that they showed others, they were somewhat reserved and loathe to show outsiders their inner feelings.

With retirement dictating a reduced income the Darbys sought to make economies. One involved the printed writing paper they had used in New York. Rather than purchase a new supply showing their Belmar address they used the simple expedient of crossing out 2706 Heath Avenue with a typewriter and substituting the New Jersey address. *11*

Darby Letter Heading.
(Ron Holz Collection.)

Such was the supply that they still had that it was to last them a number of years.

The Darbys were delighted in 1954 to learn that their former lodger and dear friend, Major William Slater, had been appointed as Bandmaster of the New York Staff Band. He was to serve a five year term in that office. There was further good news later the same year when William, who had been widowed some years earlier, married Lois Hargreaves who had been George's Assistant at the Property Department.

The author with Lois Slater, November 2001. *10*
(Photo by Debbie Danson.)

In the late 1950s, Elizabeth came down with measles. She was later to joke that this was indeed proof that she was going through her second childhood. Not long after this her health failed again and her doctors diagnosed inoperable cancer. An exploratory incision was closed up and she was allowed to go home to die, she herself being aware of this grave prognosis.

On one of their visits with Elizabeth after hearing this news, William and Lois Slater were surprised to find her standing at the dining room table separating some lovely African violets. As ever, Elizabeth was full of smiles.

"What am I supposed to do?" she asked, "Go to bed and wait until the Lord calls me?" It was obvious that Elizabeth was ready and prepared for death.

In order to facilitate her remaining at home, Mary and Floyd Freeman, who following their retirement in 1957 in the rank of Senior Major, had purchased the adjoining half of the Darbys' duplex, took over caring for Elizabeth and looked after all of her household chores. Acts of Christian family love which they were happy to carry out particularly as they may also have seen it as a way or repaying Elizabeth and George for all the kindnesses they had shown Mary when she had first arrived in America.

Attending a service at   *In the garden of their Belmar home,*
Asbury Park, August 1957.   *July 1958.*

(Ethel and Charles Edge Collections.)

Mary unexpectedly died on the 23rd September 1961 and her death meant that Elizabeth and George had to move into the Retired Officers Residence at Asbury Park, as Elizabeth had predicted, where she could receive the continuing care she required.

The Order of Service for Mary's funeral in part read: "She was a marvellous cook," Colonel Darby said of his sister, "and won the confidence of many a troubled man in the institution over her newly baked apple strudel. She revelled in service to humanity and truly was a servant of all." Since their retirement Mrs Freeman, with her husband, had taken part in

A postcard of the Salvation Army Home for Retired Officers, Asbury Park NJ.
(Author's Collection.)

the Asbury Park, N.J., Corps activities and will be missed greatly by the officers and soldiers there. The prayers and thoughts of their comrades and friends everywhere will surround Sr.-Major Freeman and his daughter Ruth, and Colonel and Mrs Darby, for whom her loss, in practical kindness, is especially great. May the God of comfort and hope sustain them all.

With the limited amount of accommodation available to Elizabeth and George within the Retirement Home it was necessary for the couple to give away many of their treasured possessions. Mimi Uricoli was given four framed paintings which had adorned Elizabeth's sitting room walls. Two of the paintings, both from originals by Jean Francois Millet, are still in the Uricoli family today:

Man With a Hoe, (1863).
(Marie Uricoli Collection.)

The Angelus (Musee d'Orsay 1863) *9*
(Francis Trojack Collection.)

Of particular joy, and strength, to Elizabeth and George in their retirement years, both at Belmar and Asbury Park, were the regular visits they received from their many friends and Raymond who would sometimes be accompanied by his two children, Jerilyn and Ray Jnr. The two grandchildren had inherited the Darby prowess for music and were both proficient clarinet players. This must have been particularly pleasing to George. Ray Lewis recalls that on one visit, his grandfather told him that their line of the Darby family were direct descendants of Admiral Sir Henry D'Esterre Darby who had commanded the *HMS Bellerophon* at the Battle of the Nile in 1798.

One of the young people at Asbury Park during the Darbys' residence there was Bandsman Lee Yvonne Hodgson whose parents, Majors Agnes and Cecil Hodgson were in Command of the Corps. Lee can recall that the juniors were invited one evening to the home of William and Lois Slater. George Darby was also there and it was a fine evening of fellowship and respect for the two senior musicians. It was from George that the juniors learned of Elizabeth's involvement with the *Titanic*. Lee once asked Elizabeth how she had managed to survive the disaster and received the short, but all-telling reply, "The Lord was with me."

Whilst at Asbury Park, Elizabeth underwent an X-ray to determine the present state of her cancer and her physicians were amazed to note that no traces of malignancy were discovered. Yet one more time Elizabeth had had a brush with death and had walked away the victor.

There was to be just one more occasion. In a letter to her nephew Clifford, dated 12th April 1961, Elizabeth wrote of a malfunction of her electric blanket which had set fire to the bed in which she had been sleeping. She awoke to find herself uninjured save for minor smoke inhalation but her nightwear was scorched.

'You remember what Uncle George said,' she wrote, 'that I wouldn't drown nor burn, he would have to shoot me.' This from a lady who, by this time, was living in constant pain and sickness, and knew that her life was drawing to its close. The same letter ended, 'And now I say, please Lord, take me Home.'

George's concern over his wife's health received one short respite in June 1962, when the NYSB celebrated its Diamond Jubilee reunion at the Seaside Hotel, Ocean Grove just a short distance away from the Retirement Home. George had been a member of the organising committee and it must have been a great delight to him to spend the weekend in the company of three other retired bandmasters and many of the bandsmen who had served under them. The humour that had existed within the band during George's tenure had obviously carried forward to the present day as the programme for the weekend contained one of the earliest pictures of the Staff Band upon which photographs of two present day members had been super-imposed!

At the 75th Band Anniversary Celebrations - a bevy of Bandmasters!
From left to right: William Bearchell (1945-1951), George Darby (1912-1931),
Charles Mehling (ex-Bandsman), William Maltby (NYSB Executive Officer
1957-1964), William Slater (1951-1955).
(Salvation Army National HQ Archives and Research Center USA.)

Prior to the formal meal on the Saturday evening, a number of speeches were made. As George was the senior member present to him went the honour of speaking last and he did so under the title, 'Words of Wisdom' - a collection of the anecdotes which had insured his popularity over the years. Just prior to the meal the entire company joined in singing, *"Bread of Heaven"* with George conducting his beloved band. We can be certain that the tears also welled in his eyes on this occasion, conducting the NYSB again at the age of 79. At the end of the evening the entire Darby family were asked to stand and they received tumultuous applause from all those present. Ray Lewis was old enough to realise that this was a sign of the great affection in which his grandparents were held.

Elizabeth Darby was promoted to Glory in the early hours of 22nd November 1963 at the age of 81, at the Salvation Army Retired Officers Residence. Later the same day, John Fitzgerald Kennedy, 35th President of the United States of America, was slain in Dallas, Texas. The following day's edition of *The New York Times* reported the death of the President and on page 29 carried an obituary for Elizabeth Darby.

Elizabeth's funeral service was held on Sunday 24th November at the Asbury Park Temple and the service was conducted by the National

Commander, Commissioner Holland French. Lee Hodgson, now Mrs DeMoranville, played in the senior band during the service. At its conclusion the band formed a line outside the hall and played hymns as the Salvation Army flag was marched out. This was followed by Elizabeth's casket and the family mourners.

The Order of Service for Elizabeth's funeral contained the following eulogy;

MRS. COLONEL GEORGE DARBY (R)

The Salvation Army became the poorer on Friday morning, November 22, when, after a long life of kind deeds and unusual goodness, Mrs. Colonel George Darby slipped peacefully away to continue life among the redeemed in the Eternal City. Death held no terror for her, for she lived heroically and well.

Born in Folkestone, England on May 27, 1882, Mrs. Darby was a life-long Salvationist. From earliest childhood there was set before her by her parents examples of lives governed by the principles of self-sacrifice and service as opposed to self-seeking and pleasure. (Her father was the organizer of the Folkestone Corps and was its first bandmaster.) Such Christlikeness made a deep impression upon her, and in due time she decided to chart a career of service.

She came to the United States some years later, entered the Salvation Army School for Officers' Training in New York City, was commissioned an officer in 1913, and was married to the then Captain Darby the same year.

Mrs. Darby was a woman of deep religious convictions and high principles. She was not demonstrative. She was not a gifted platform personality, but with her calm and serene spirit, and in her quiet and unobtrusive way, she accomplished much for God and The Army in those behind-the-scenes activities which fall to the lot of so many Savationist women.

Particularly effective was her service rendered

through Home League and League of Mercy ministry in the New York area, where she spent her entire active career. She revelled in such work and revealed unsuspected resources and capacities. Ungrudgingly, she gave her strength to the weak, her substance to the poor, her sympathy to the suffering, and, moreover, gave it with a graciousness which added much to its influence. Thousands of people whom she met during this period will treasure in their hearts her many spontaneous acts of kindness and helpfulness, and will keep her memory green.

Mrs. Darby was one of the few survivors of the *Titanic* disaster in 1912.

The tender and prayerful sympathy of Salvationists and friends everywhere will be extended to Colonel Darby and to the son, George Ray.

Elizabeth was interred on the 25th November at Kensico Cemetery, Valhalla, just a short distance from the grave of General Evangeline Booth. The service ended with the playing of TAPS.

Elizabeth's passing was also marked by a report in *The Folkestone Herald* of 7th December, which detailed her upbringing in Folkestone and continued, '*A staunch Salvationist all her life, Mrs Darby gave long and tireless service to the Army. Her father was the first bandmaster of Folkestone Salvation Army Corps, and her husband, Salvation Army Colonel George Darby, now retired, was bandmaster of New York Staff Band for a great number of years.*

Sailing to America on the ill-fated RMS Titanic *on April 10th 1912, Mrs Darby was one of the few survivors. Her bravery following the disaster and her long fight against the consequent shock and exposure were, in themselves, a tribute to a strong and heroic character, but the anguished memories of that fateful night remained to haunt her throughout her life.*

Mrs Darby resided in America for over 50 years yet never lost touch with her family and friends in Folkestone, nor did she ever lose interest in her hometown, its changes and developments. Perhaps her greatest wish, voiced often in her later years, was to walk again in springtime through the lanes and see the English countryside, and particularly the primroses and bluebells. Alas, ill-health prevented the fulfilment of that wish.

Order of Service

At the Funeral of

MRS. COLONEL GEORGE DARBY (R)

Sunday, November 24, 1963
2:30 p.m.

Conducted by

COMMISSIONER HOLLAND FRENCH
National Commander

The Salvation Army Temple
510 Grand Avenue
Asbury Park, New Jersey

The Order of Service for Elizabeth Darby's funeral.

Mrs Darby is survived by her husband and son, and by three sisters resident in Folkestone who mourn her passing.'

George Darby remained at the Retired Officers Residence after Elizabeth's death. Understandably he felt lonely and would sometimes walk the mile or so distance to the retirement home in Ocean Grove, of William and Lois Slater. There he would eat a meal and then enjoy relaxing in the company of dear friends. George continued to be a faithful soldier

The report featured in 'The Folkestone Herald' of 7th December, 1963.

Survivor Of The "Titanic" Sea Disaster FH.7¹²/₆₃

Mrs. E. Darby.

Army Corps, and her husband, Salvation Army Colonel George Darby, now retired, was Bandmaster of New York Staff Band for a great number of years.

Sailing to America on the ill-fated R.M.S. *Titanic* on April 10th, 1912, Mrs. Darby was one of the few survivors.

BRAVE WOMAN

Her bravery following the disaster and her long fight against the consequent ill-health caused by shock and exposure were in themselves a tribute to a strong and heroic character, but the anguished memories of that fateful night remained to haunt her throughout her life.

Mrs. Darby resided in America for over 50 years yet never lost touch with her family and friends in Folkestone, nor did she ever lose interest in her home town, its changes and developments.

HER WISH

Perhaps her greatest wish, voiced often in her later years, was to walk again in Springtime through the lanes and woods of her beloved Kent and see the English countryside, and particularly, the primroses and bluebells.

Alas, ill-health prevented the fulfilment of that wish.

Mrs. Darby is survived by her husband and son, and by three sisters resident in Folkestone who mourn her passing.

THE death occurred recently at Asbury Park, New Jersey, U.S.A., of Mrs. Elizabeth Darby, 81, eldest daughter of the late Mr. and Mrs. Thomas Ramell, whom older Folkestone residents will remember as owners of a coachbuilding business in Dover Road.

As a child, Mrs. Darby attended Dover Road Board School, now Hillside Secondary Modern. From there she went to work for Musgrave and Co. Ltd., late of Sandgate Road, where she remained for many years.

A staunch Salvationist all her life, Mrs. Darby gave long and tireless service to the "Army." Her father was the first Bandmaster of Folkestone Salvation

Vandals ⟵

The Order of Service for George Darby's funeral.
(Salvation Army National HQ Archives and Research Centre USA.)

of the Asbury Park Corps and took a particular interest in young people. Not content to approve from afar, he was often found to be in the bandroom, expressing his appreciation of their performance and when the young peoples' singing company needed uniforms, it was Colonel Darby who saw that their needs were met. He was also promoted to Glory from the Residence on 7th May 1968, at the age of 84. After a funeral conducted by his old and dear friend William Slater, George was interned with Elizabeth at Valhalla.

In time, a grey granite headstone joined the uniform rows of markers commemorating the fallen warriors of the Salvation Army. The inscription reads:

DARBY
Colonel ELIZABETH 1882-1963
Colonel GEORGE 1883-1968
Gallant Christian Pilgrims

EPILOGUE

Elizabeth's story however does not end with her death.

On the 1st September 1985, the wreck of the *Titanic* was located by a joint USA/French expedition headed by Dr Robert Ballard. In 1912 there had been just a small number of survivors, like Elizabeth, who thought that the *Titanic* had split in two on sinking, but the general consensus was that she had not. The discovery of the wreck was to confirm the minority view had been correct and that she had parted.

In 1987, amid great controversy, an expedition financed by Titanic Ventures (later succeeded by *RMS Titanic* Inc) started recovery operations of items from the debris area between the two main parts of the wreck. One of the early items to be recovered was a decorative white porcelain watering can, pristine in condition except that the handle is missing. The item is emblazoned with gold lettering reading, 'A Present From Folkestone'.

Identical, but intact, watering can as found on the seabed.
(Author's Collection.)

There can be no other likely explanation for the presence of this seaside souvenir on the *Titanic*, other than it came from the luggage of Elizabeth Nye and was being taken back to America by her as a reminder of home. The watering can now forms part of a touring exhibition which premiered in Europe in 1989 and is now currently touring major cities throughout the United States.

On Sunday, 23rd March 1997, I visited Elizabeth and George's grave at the tranquil and very beautiful setting of Kensico Cemetery. By the graveside, primroses were placed bearing the simple inscription:

For Lizzie - A Present From Folkestone.

A shorter version of this biography of Elizabeth Nye first appeared in print in Vol 21 - 3rd Quarter, November 97 - January 98 edition of *The Titanic Commutator*, Official Journal of the Titanic Historical Society, MA USA.

Appendix I

1. Following Elizabeth's death in 1963 the Bible, which had remained in England, was bequeathed to Clifford Greene. He, in turn, passed it to his good friend Mrs Edna Hart who, after Clifford's own death in 1999, knowing of my interest in Elizabeth, very kindly gave the Bible to me. I treasure it as a very valuable link to Elizabeth Nye.

2. Miss Russell died in April 1975 at the age of 98 and the musical pig was bequeathed to Walter Lord. Displaying a humour similar to Elizabeth's, Miss Russell once remarked of herself, "I'm accident prone. I've been in shipwrecks, car crashes, fires, floods and tornadoes. I've had every disaster but bubonic plague and a husband!" When I visited Mr Lord in his New York apartment in March 1997, he very kindly showed me the musical pig.

3. When Leah Aks, the mother of the baby, Frank Aks, was also rescued by the *Carpathia* she frantically searched aboard the vessel for her son. At last she recognised him in the arms of another woman who claimed that the child was her own. The matter was only resolved by taking the dispute before Captain Rostron and Leah Aks stating that her son had a birthmark. This was confirmed and Frank was returned to her. In his later life Frank Aks was to lecture on the subject of the *Titanic* and claim that the woman who tried to keep him was Elizabeth Nye. This scurrilous story has appeared in at least two books about the *Titanic* disaster, on a number of websites and even Passenger Display Boards at Titanic Exhibitions. I am indebted to Ed and Karen Kamuda of the Titanic Historical Society who were able to trace a number of 1912 press cuttings and other references in which Leah Aks clearly states that the woman who tried to keep her son was Italian and had been widowed in the disaster. This is clearly not a description of Elizabeth. Frank Aks died in 1991 at the age of 80.

4. Rosa Abbott was a 35 year old Salvationist originally from St. Albans, Hertfordshire, who had been returning to the United States aboard the Titanic with her two sons, Rossmore 16, and Eugene 13. There are differing accounts of her departure from the *Titanic*; all that is certain is that neither of her sons survived. Rosa remarried in 1912 and was last heard of living in Florida.

5. In the late 1970s, Thomas Ramell, as Bandmaster Tom, was immortalised in the musical, 'GLORY', which tells the story of the early days of the Folkestone Corps. The musical was written by two young

Salvation Army Officers, John Gowans and John Larsson. Between May 1999 and November 2002, General John Gowans commanded the Salvation Army worldwide. I am indebted to the General for his continuing particular interest in stories about the Folkestone Corps and for kindly agreeing to write the foreword to this book. John Gowans was succeeded as General by John Larsson.

6. Sadly, Ray George Darby was forced into an early retirement due to the onset of bad health. He died on 7th November 1979. He was survived by his wife and two children. A new Science Block built at Fieldston School after his death was named in his memory.

7. On his return to the UK, Ron Darby was commissioned and spent the rest of the war flying Fairey Swordfish aircraft with 836 Sqn on the Atlantic patrol. At the end of the war he returned to Cannock and took up teaching for the next 40 years. He is now in retirement and remains a fit and active septuagenarian.

8. Following the death of Thomas Ramell, his wife continued to run the carriage works until forced by the overwhelming competition from motor vehicles, to shut down in 1928. Elizabeth Ramell died in 1947 at the age of 93. Her interment was to reunite her with Thomas. She left one-sixth of her estate to each of her five daughters and one granddaughter.

9. By a remarkable, and happy, coincidence the author has had a copy of the same painting hanging in his own sitting room for the last twenty years.

10. I would not consider these notes complete without a mention of, and thanks for, the extravagance of the welcome accorded to Debbie and I by the Uricoli family on a visit we made in November 2001 to their home in New Jersey. On the same trip we were also delighted to meet up with Ruth E. Freeman and Lois Slater, two charming ladies.

11. 2706 Heath Avenue still stands in the Bronx and many of the interior fixtures and fittings, unbelievably, remain the same as when the Darbys lived there. The dining room on the middle floor still has the oak beams and wall panelling, the front room has the original dark wood fireplace and surround, and the kitchen wall and workspace tiles all still date from the 1920s. I am grateful to the present owner, Ezequiel Hernandez, and the present middle floor tenant Cynthia Ortega, for the unrestricted access they allowed me to the house. In the cellar we found the original cage for the dumbwaiter. I felt very close to Elizabeth whilst I was there.

Appendix II

So many people have kindly helped over the years with information, photographs, personal reminiscences and documents that I have filled six complete box files with their generous contributions. Those I have to thank are;

In the UK:

Salvation Army Personnel: General John Gowans, Major Helen Bryden, Major and Mrs Graham Grayston, Major David Lewis, Lt Col Joan Williams (R), Major David Dalziel, Pam and Tony Barr.

and

Penny Bearman, Shane Beatty, Winifred Beckett, Dr. Gary D. Calver, Rachel Clark, Sonia Clifton, Lynn P. Cook, Jack M. Dalton (since deceased), John Dalton, Debbie Danson, Ron Darby, Charles and Ethel Edge, Kerry Emery, John Fry, Ernie Fuggle, Anne Gibson, Clifford Greene (since deceased), Gemma Griffiths, Janet Guy, Edna Hart, Brenda Hearnden, Wendy Hiles, Philip Hind, Rebecca Hine, Peter Hooper, John K. Hughes, Roger Ivens, Levina Jones, Alan Lord, Russell Lord, William MacQuitty, David Miller, Simon Mills, Mick Milton, Adrian and Chris Munnings, Julian Perez, Alice and Joanne Pickering, Jeanne Punnett, Alan Ramell, Geoff Robinson, Somer Rogers, Lisa Smith, Angela Staker, Ebony Staker, Taziella Staker, Maxine Stanley, Douglas Sulley, Emma Tate, Alan and Eileen Taylor, Gordon Taylor, Brian Ticehurst, Steve Walker, Geoff Whitfield, Len and Doreen Williams, Dave Wise and the ever patient staff at the Folkestone Library Heritage Centre.

In Australia and New Zealand:

Inger Sheil, June Fuger, Mary Pellett.

In the USA and Canada:

Salvation Army Personnel: Major Barbara Bawks, Ruth E. Freeman, Lt Col Alice Joyce, Col Lois Slater (R), Lee DeMoranville.

and

Deborah Amadei, Carol D'Arpa, Jim Avey, Jack Eaton, Calicia Fountain, Anne Francis, Macie Garr, Phillip Gowan, John and Vera Gillespie, Ezequiel Hernandez, Charlie Haas, Toby Himmel, Dr. Ronald W. Holz Ph.D., Alice Joyce, Ed and Karen Kamuda, Walter Lord (since deceased), Brian Meister, Susan Mitchem, Cynthia Ortega, Jean-Paul Picard, Bob

Pringle, Eric S. Robinson, Grace Roper, Dana Smith, Karen L. Schnitzspahn, Francis Trojack, Mimi and Biaggio Uricoli, Beverly Vaillancourt, Robert Wagner, Dawn and Robert Wolfenbarger, Shelia Williams and not forgetting Anne Williams who swept away the leaves before I took some of the photographs!

My sincere thanks to them all - and to anyone else whose name may inadvertently still be buried in one of the box files!

APPENDIX III

SELECTED BIBLIOGRAPHY

Herbert A. Wisbey Jr., 'Soldiers Without Swords' *(The MacMillan Company)*

Cyril Barnes, 'Booth's England' *(Egon Publishers Ltd)*

Sallie Chesham, 'Born To Battle' *(The Salvation Army NY, NY)*

Edward H. Joy, 'The Old Corps' *(Salvationist Publishing and Supplies Ltd)*

Ronald W. Holz, 'Heralds of Victory' *(The Salvation Army Literary Department)*

Karen L. Schnitzspahn, 'Images of America - Belmar' *(Arcadia Publishing)*

Walter Lord, 'A Night To Remember' *(Penguin)*

Walter Lord, 'The Night Lives On' *(Viking)*

John P. Eaton, Charles A. Haas, 'Titanic Destination Disaster' *(Patrick Stephens Ltd)*

W. A. Parks M.Sc., 'The Story of Dover Road School' *(Parsons)*

'Loss of the SS Titanic Court of Enquiry' *(PRO Publications)*

Eric Caren & Steve Goldman, 'Titanic, The Story of the Disaster in the Newspapers of the Day' *(Bayman Press)*

'Titanic Disaster Hearings' *(Washington Government Printing Office)*

Maxwell Ryan, 'The Canadian Campaign' *(Salvation Army Publications)*

OTHER SOURCES:

The War Cry, UK and USA Editions

The Commutator, 'Quarterly journal of the Titanic Historical Society Inc.'

PO Box 51053, Indian Orchard, MA 01151-0053 USA
Email: titanicinfo@titanic1.org Website: www.titanic1.org

Atlantic Daily Bulletin, 'Quarterly journal of the British Titanic Society'

PO Box 401, Hope Carr Way, Leigh, Lancs WN7 3WW, UK

APPENDIX IV

Much of the information about George Darby's early years in Cannock, Staffordshire is taken from writings by his sister Mary, penned in 1938. These were found amongst her possession by her daughter Ruth, after her death in 1961. Her reflections are a wonderful piece of prose and I am most grateful that Ruth has kindly allowed me to reproduce the work here in its entirety.

**Rumer Hill
Cannock
Staffordshire
England**

**Memories of the Old Home and my
Childhood Days.**

I see a hill, a Cottage and a winding path to the door.
I smell the sweet fragrance of the honeysuckle
round the windows
I see a wild cherry tree bursting forth with bloom,
It is Spring.

I see a pool of sparkling water,
Beautiful green fields and wild flowers,
I see a lovely garden with fruit trees, and vegetables
and flowers.

Look! I see ducks swimming on the pool
I hear the pigs in the pen, they are squealing for
their meal,
I see the chickens running around.

This was the place of my birth, also the birthplace of my father.
Not a mansion, but a cottage where love and joy doth abide.
The place where I grew up as a young girl, with my brothers and sisters.
The place where I spent many happy hours.

I think of the old lanes and beautiful woods we used to romp through.
Gathering bluebells and all kinds of wild flowers.

In the tall trees in the distance I hear the cuckoo.
I see coming down the old lane a flock of sheep and lambs.
They are going to the meadow.
I see a spring of water, clear as crystal.
I fill my pails and take it home.

I think of the berrying season when we used to take our quart jugs and gather the blackberries,
I think of the fishing in the pool in the Summer,
And the fun we had skating in the winter.
Yes these certainly were happy days.

But listen, I hear the strains of music,
That must be George playing on his euphonium.
What is that he is playing? 'Annie Laurie'.
It is very quiet and still outside and as I listen I hear the echo full and clear.

Who do I see now?
It is old Granny with her white hair and little black bonnet.
She is sitting out under the cherry tree.
Shelling the peas and cutting the beans for Sunday dinner.

I remember the lickings we got from old Gran, but
we deserved them.
The next minute she would be telling us to look in
the bottom of the old clock in her bedroom
And we would find a penny.
Old Gran was alright, one of the best.
Helped to take care of us when we were small.
I can see her now sitting in the old armchair,
The little black bonnet on her head.

I think of the old school house on Walsall Road.
Listen! I hear the bell. Ding dong, ding dong, ding
dong.
Now children get your hats and coats on, it is time
for school.

Well, here comes old scamp (the dog),
His ear half gone, and only one eye through which
he can see.
He's been in a fight again.
Poor old fellow, he was always ready for a fight.
I will never forget the grave we made for him
And the headstone with the words written on 'Gone
but not forgotten'

There goes Harry for a swim in the pool.
In he dives, will he ever come up again? Oh I am
scared.
Here he comes with that famous breaststroke, now
he is doing sidestroke,
Now backstroke, isn't he clever?

Look, there goes Dad and George and Harry along
the path.
They have their instruments under their arms.
They are off to the Army.

I see old Cruger the old black and white cat fast
asleep on the hearth.
I hear the kettle singing on the old grate.
It is getting near teatime.
The old thrush in the cage hanging on the wall sings
a few notes.

What is that now I hear? It is the threshing machine
in the old farmyard
They are gathering in the corn from the fields.
It is harvest time.

In the distance I see the old cowshed.
I see the cows grazing in the field. Some are lying
around chewing the cud.
There goes a mother horse and a little colt.
I hear the birds singing in the trees.
It has been a hot day.

I see the cattle come down to the pool to drink.
Get your pails ready we will have to carry water
from the old pool to water the flowers and
vegetables.
Oh, I am glad it is over with, my back aches carrying
those pails of water.

Oh what excitement! George is getting a new horn.
A beautiful silver and gold plated euphonium.
It is coming, I see the men bringing it in, my what a
big package.
It is so big it will scarcely come through the door.
Will we ever get it opened up such a lot of nails to
take out and such a lot of straw and packaging.
Oh, here it comes, isn't it beautiful and what a rich
tone it has.
"I will name it Rex". I remember, do you George?

I hear music. That is George and Harry in the parlour going over a new piece.

"Watch out for your time our kid. Look out for that F Sharp, and watch the B Flat."

"1 2 3 4, that was pretty good, but I think we can do better." So they try again.

It is Saturday afternoon. I see George sitting at the old kitchen table with his euphonium.

He is going to practise "Moll", he said, calling me by my nickname.

"Bring me a jug of water. Now I am all set and ready for work."

Up the scale and down the scale he goes.

Now for some old pieces. I hear 'Annie Laurie, Robin Adair, Should Old Aquaintance be Forgot' and 'Home Sweet Home.'

I see an old pen at the back of the house where we used to keep our bikes,

Where George and Harry spent many happy hours playing with the little steam engine Dad and Mother bought for them.

My, can't that little engine work! Harry lets off the steam, he gives a loud whistle.

Now she is going, just watch her.

We are sitting around the fire in the parlour, it is Christmas Eve.

It is snowing and a north wind is blowing, but listen, I hear singing.

Why, that is Dad outside singing us a Christmas carol. He just got home from open air.

What is he singing? Listen again, 'Christians Awake' Yum, yum. I smell plum pudding and look at that plate of home made mincepies.

Don't they look good?

It is early Christmas morning.
I see several stockings hanging filled with oranges, apples, nuts and sweets.
Santa Claus must have been.
I see the kitchen table and all the toys.
I see a doll for me with golden curls and blue eyes.
Oh the thrill of those Christmas mornings, I will never forget.
I see Dad's stocking hanging there filled too, I won't say with what.
But never mind it was a lot of fun.
It certainly brings back to my mind sweet memories of childhood days.

Now I see a little frail woman with greying hair - my Mother.
Busying herself with the many household duties of the home and family.
Ever mindful of her children and their needs. What wonderful patience and courage she had.
What a wonderful mother.

It is six o'clock. Here comes Dad home from work after his hard day's work.
He was always such a good father, a good provider and a wonderful example to his family.

But this one time, home of joy and comfort with good parents has passed.
In it's place stands a towering mould of earth and stone dug up from the depths of the earth.
To one side stands a great mountain of coal shining and glittering in the sun like huge diamonds.
To the other side stands the magnificent pit head modernly equipped with baths for the miners to wash.

Swift to its close. Ebbs out life's little day.
Earth joys grow dim. Its glories pass away.
Change and decay. In all around I see
Oh, Thou, who changest not - Abide with me.

Mary Darby Freeman

Written January 21st, in the year of 1938.
In memory of the old home stead and my parents.